WHO IS MY NEIGHBOUR?

T0327122

Cover images

The cover images are taken from *The Stations*, by Marksteen Adamson.

The Stations traces the emotional journey of refugees, provoking reflection and daring response. Drawing on the emotional suffering represented by the traditional 14 'Stations of the Cross', it encapsulates the experiences and stories of refugees as they embark on a harrowing emotional as well as geographical journey.

The Stations reinterprets an ancient series of images which have spoken for centuries to those who have experienced pain and desolation. Christ's journey of suffering is a universal one, played out in the suffering of people from different faith backgrounds, captured through stories and pictures of a modern humanitarian crisis. Marksteen Adamson spent a lot of time in the Calais Jungle camp and travelled to Beqaa Valley (on the border of Syria) in Lebanon to find the source of the refugee crisis, and to discover and document the individual stories he heard, which eventually informed this project.

The two images on the cover of this book are part of a touring exhibition which was launched at St Martin-in-the-Fields (see <http://thestations.org.uk/>).

Front cover: A kiss of peace between playmates in a camp for Syrian refugees.

Back cover: A young man stands at the border fence of the Jungle looking at the trucks as they go on their way to the port and on to the UK.

All photography: Marksteen Adamson © 2016.

WHO IS MY NEIGHBOUR?

The global and personal challenge

Edited by
Richard Carter and Samuel Wells

First published in Great Britain in 2018

Society for Promoting Christian Knowledge
36 Causton Street
London SW1P 4ST
www.spck.org.uk

Copyright © Richard Carter and Samuel Wells 2018

All rights reserved. No part of this book may be reproduced or transmitted in any
form or by any means, electronic or mechanical, including photocopying,
recording, or by any information storage and retrieval system,
without permission in writing from the publisher.

SPCK does not necessarily endorse the individual views contained
in its publications.

The author and publisher have made every effort to ensure that the external website
and email addresses included in this book are correct and up to date at the time
of going to press. The author and publisher are not responsible for the content,
quality or continuing accessibility of the sites.

Unless otherwise noted, Scripture quotations are taken from the New Revised
Standard Version of the Bible, Anglicized Edition, copyright © 1989, 1995 by the
Division of Christian Education of the National Council of the Churches of
Christ in the USA. Used by permission. All rights reserved.
The quotations in Chapter 7 are the author's own translation.

The publisher and authors acknowledge with thanks permission to reproduce
extracts from the following:
'You, Neighbor God', by Rainer Maria Rilke, translated by Babette Deutch, from
Poems from the Book of Hours, copyright © 1941 by New Directions Publishing
Corp. Reprinted by permission of New Directions Publishing Corp.
Every effort has been made to seek permission to use copyright material
reproduced in this book. The publisher apologizes for those cases where permission
might not have been sought and, if notified, will formally seek permission at the
earliest opportunity.

British Library Cataloguing-in-Publication Data
A catalogue record for this book is available from the British Library

ISBN 978–0–281–07840–0
eBook ISBN 978–0–281–07841–7

Typeset by Manila Typesetting Company

eBook by Manila Typesetting Company

Produced on paper from sustainable forests

For members of the
Sunday International Group
at St Martin-in-the-Fields

Contents

A note on contributors

Shulamit Ambalu is Principal Rabbi at Sha'arei Tsedek North London Reform Synagogue and is a lecturer at Leo Baeck College, London.

Luke Bretherton is Professor of Theological Ethics at Duke University, North Carolina.

Richard Carter is Associate Vicar for Mission at St Martin-in-the-Fields.

Sarah Coakley is the Norris-Hulse Professor of Divinity at the University of Cambridge.

Brendan Cox is an aid worker and former adviser on international development to Prime Minister Gordon Brown. His wife, the MP Jo Cox, was murdered in her Batley and Spen constituency in West Yorkshire in June 2016.

Stanley Hauerwas is the Gilbert T. Rowe Professor Emeritus of Divinity and Law at Duke University, North Carolina.

Michael Northcott is Professor of Ethics in the School of Divinity at the University of Edinburgh.

Anna Rowlands is the St Hilda Associate Professor of Catholic Social Thought and Practice in the Department of Theology and Religion at the Durham University.

Sarah Teather is Director of the Jesuit Refugee Service UK and is a former Liberal Democrat MP and Minister of State for Children and Families.

Megan Warner is Postdoctoral Researcher in the Department
of Theology and Religion at the University of Exeter.
Justin Welby is Archbishop of Canterbury.
Samuel Wells is Vicar of St Martin-in-the-Fields and Visiting
Professor of Christian Ethics at King's College, London.
Rowan Williams is Master of Magdalene College, Cambridge.
He was previously Archbishop of Canterbury.

Preface

This is a book about migration. But because it's about migration it's about cross-cultural relationships, fear, discovery, surprises, politics and faith. Which are what the Bible is about. So it turns out to be a book about the renewal of Christianity and the Church in the face of what seems to be a crisis but might turn out to be a gift. Or many millions of gifts.

St Martin-in-the-Fields is located at the point of the highest density of homeless people in Europe (5 per cent of those who sleep outside in Britain bed down on the Strand). We are experiencing extraordinary movements of people, movements that reflect the political, climatic, social and economic changes affecting our continent and world. In the autumn of 2016 St Martin's hosted a series of lectures entitled 'Who is My Neighbour? The Ethics of Global Relationships'. The chapters in this book arose out of those lectures and from conversations that accompanied and were related to them. We are grateful to members of the Education Group and many other supportive heads, hands and hearts at St Martin-in-the-Fields who made those lectures such wonderful events.

We invited a mixture of academics, practitioners, politicians, clergy and active citizens to contribute to this book.

We are glad of the diversity of background, perception and style of writing that the completed volume represents.

We are especially grateful to Canterbury Press and to Church Publishing for kind permission to include the chapter 'Remember you were a stranger', which was previously published as 'Migration' in Samuel Wells, *How Then Shall We Live? Christian Engagement with Contemporary Issues* (Norwich: Canterbury Press, 2016/New York: Church Publishing, 2017); and to Eerdmans and again to Canterbury Press for kind permission to publish the chapter 'My neighbour, God's gift', a different form of which was previously published as 'Being with the neighbour' in Samuel Wells, *Incarnational Mission: Being with the World* (Grand Rapids, MI: Eerdmans/Norwich: Canterbury Press, 2018). Anna Rowlands' chapter first appeared at <www.abc.net.au/religion/articles/2016/06/29/4491205.htm>.

The book is dedicated to several dozen remarkable and brave people who have for the last five years now been involved in our Sunday International Group and whose stories, if ever fully told, would move, inspire and humble all who heard them and would surely transform the public discourse around the stranger.

Prologue: Remember you were a stranger

Samuel Wells

There's perhaps no issue today where the Church's understanding of God and the momentum of public opinion are as far apart as they are on immigration. I want to explore how this demanding issue can be a source of renewal for Church and nation.

Around 230 million people, more than 3 per cent of the world's population, are currently migrants. About one-fifth of that number have travelled beyond their region of origin. There are different names for migrants: those who choose or are forced to flee from desperate situations and request settlement in a new country we call asylum seekers; those who are accepted in the new country we call refugees; those who are forced out of a country but aren't in an application process we call displaced persons; those whose applications aren't accepted we call failed asylum seekers; those who are simply seeking a better life, sometimes in the face of destitution, we usually call economic migrants. Often these distinctions break down. In general, migrants are driven by political or economic aspiration – or more often desperation.

Such desperation is increasing for a number of reasons. The political reasons mostly concern war and persecution: unrest or oppression in Syria, Eritrea, Zimbabwe, Colombia,

Afghanistan, Democratic Republic of the Congo and Somalia, some of it exacerbated by the end of the Cold War, has generated a huge number of refugees. Economic factors include poverty, environmental crisis, and the inequalities exacerbated by globalization; economic considerations also affect those drawn to the West for better work and welfare prospects. Meanwhile the expansion of the European Union has created an ambiguity in Europe about what is regarded as migration. Social dimensions involve the presence of relatives already based elsewhere and the emergence of an industry of trafficking and smuggling.

This significant displacement of populations is at root the fallout of the global political and economic system. Western governments retain their electoral legitimacy by preserving a global climate of trade and security. But that global climate has casualties. Migrants are the flotsam and jetsam of the ocean wave of global power. And the perceived crisis over migration arises from the assumption of Western governments and populations that the only way to deal with the symptoms of this global fallout is to shoo people away as much as possible for as long as possible.

Since September 11, 2001 there's been a lurking fear that somehow the most antagonized citizens of the Global South are poised to take revenge on the West for its real or perceived neocolonial sins. The paradox of the migration issue is that, in the Western popular imagination, migrants, in other words those most hurt by and vulnerable to the shortcomings of their countries of origin, become the visible embodiment of these terrifying risks that seem to have no limits or borders; and when that small minority of migrants actually make it through the system and are settled, for example, in the UK, they can find themselves side by side with hurt and vulnerable people in some of the most challenging neighbourhoods in the country. Thus the anxieties of both incoming and host populations are almost inevitably exacerbated and the issue becomes more fraught than it might otherwise be.

Before we go any further, let's identify and dispel a few influential but inaccurate myths about migration. Neither Britain nor the USA is, or ever has been, a pure nation of a single race or religion, of everlasting regional and class harmony. Their respective borders have long been debated and permeable and they have always been a mongrel people of diverse origins. At the same time, migration is invariably a matter of mixed motives. If economic drivers were the only issue, people all over the world would be on the move all the time; yet for most people habit and familiarity and family and local networks far outweigh simple economic improvement. On the other hand, there's nothing wrong with someone who's not persecuted seeking to better themselves economically in a new country. A great many of this nation's most dynamic leaders and shapers have been immigrants or children of immigrants; for America, such a story is part of the 'founding myth' of the nation.

There isn't a simple answer to the displacement of populations. The UK and USA have much in terms of skills, culture and dynamism to gain from an influx of resourceful and community-minded new citizens – not least to rectify the imbalance of age-bands between working and retired populations. But large-scale assimilation is demanding for all concerned. It's no use naively maintaining that the government should simply remove all border controls. One unplanned side effect of such action would be to encourage oppressive regimes to feel that they could simply export their opponents to the West. The so-called IS would be delighted to do that right now.

Likewise it's not that all fears expressed among local host populations are unreasonable. There's widespread resentment that asylum seekers displace host residents in what sometimes seems a tight competition for housing, jobs, benefits and healthcare. Once again migrants become the flashpoint of existing social tensions about taxation and welfare provision and shortage of housing. The tensions are real, and the presence of asylum seekers exacerbates those tensions. But the myth is that migration is really the issue. The truth is that the tensions would be there without the asylum seekers, and the anxieties wouldn't go away if the asylum seekers went away. Those who have commercial and political capital to make out of scapegoating the stranger and fomenting a climate of fear set about fanning such anxieties even in neighbourhoods where they are groundless. A modest influx of migrants certainly changes a culture; but culture has always been changing and there's no evidence that migrants change culture for the worse by any of the conventional evaluative yardsticks.

When it comes to the churches' existing response to immigration, there are some very good things to be said and one difficult thing. The very good things are a wide range of initiatives that receive the stranger as a gift and look for the face of Christ in those that are hungry and naked and in many cases more or less in prison. Many projects offer welcome, hospitality, companionship and support; some give advice, or practical help such as clothing, food parcels, nappies and cash. Some advocate around immigration policy on a national level, seek to change attitudes more locally, or take up the cause of individuals who have had their cases neglected or rejected. And many churches have found migrants joining their congregations and enriching their liturgies and educational programmes and deepening their understanding of scriptural stories like those of the itinerant Abraham and the refugee Hagar. All these dimensions are part of our experience at my own church, St Martin's, too. The difficult thing to say is that the churches seem no closer than anyone else to being able to articulate a humane and sustainable immigration policy of which Church and nation may be proud rather than ashamed. In the absence of such a proposal, valuable church initiatives are like absorbing episodes in a drama with no overall narrative.

How might we begin to put such a proposal together? For Christians the place to begin is to alter the perception that being a migrant is something unusual or unnatural. Jesus is a displaced person in three senses. Fundamentally, he is the heavenly one who sojourned on earth. And it didn't go well: as John's Gospel puts it, 'He came to what was his own, and his own people did not accept him' (John 1.11). Then he finds himself a refugee in Egypt, his parents fleeing Herod's persecution. Third, he spends his ministry as an itinerant preacher and healer, with nowhere to lay his head. Meanwhile the story of Israel is one of migration from beginning to end. Adam and Eve leave the Garden; Noah and family sail away from destruction; Abraham follows God's call; Joseph and family head down to Egypt; Moses leads the people back; Judah is taken into exile in Babylon; Ezra and Nehemiah tell of the return. None of these people were going on a package holiday: they were refugees, asylum seekers, or trafficked persons. There is precisely one verse commanding the children of Israel, 'You shall love your neighbour as yourself'; there are no fewer than 36 verses saying 'love the stranger': care of the alien is how Israel remembers its history with gratitude.[1]

What this is telling us is that being displaced is an integral part of the whole story of the Bible, an inherent part of being God's people. Over and again we're shown lessons the people of God would never have learnt without their displacements. Israel was formed by 40 years in the wilderness and was renewed by 50 years in exile. There's no Old Testament without migration. In the New Testament, the Acts of the Apostles in general and the ministry of Paul in particular comprise one journey after another. And ultimately, as the book of Revelation makes clear, we're all in exile from our true and final abode in heaven. The sooner we realize that here we have no abiding city and that we're strangers and pilgrims on earth, the better we'll grasp the gospel. We're all travellers, like it or not. Christians can never blandly talk of migrants as 'them' and host populations as 'us'. To be a Christian is to be en route. Christians have a citizenship, but it's not situated right here.

Let me focus down on one particular migrant we may take as representative of the whole story. The crucial point about the story of Ruth is that the needy migrant becomes the source of national renewal.[2] This tiny story, almost entirely made up of dialogue, epitomizes the journey about immigration we need to make today. The backdrop is of political and environmental crisis in Israel during the time of the judges: the rule of law had been practically abandoned, and famine menaced the land. The people of Israel were sworn enemies of the Moabites, because the Moabites were seen as the fruit of incest between Lot and his daughters, and because they had refused to help Moses and his people when they themselves were strangers in the wilderness. Around 15 times in four chapters we're told that Ruth is a foreigner or a Moabitess. Ruth is like an archetypal asylum seeker today: a sexually dangerous woman from a suspicious country with a foreign religion bringing a basketload of trouble. It turns out that she is the bringer of salvation: her son Obed is set to become the grandfather of David, Israel's greatest king.

The story hinges on two face-to-face relationships: the sympathy between the Israelite widow Naomi and her daughter-in-law the Moabite widow Ruth, and the reciprocity between the same Moabitess Ruth and the wealthy but childless kinsman Boaz. Ruth faces isolation as a foreign widow amid a famine; she's vulnerable to being molested in the barley field and begins the story facing humiliation and death. But she pledges her loyalty to Naomi, now and for ever, and she matches her impoverishment with Boaz's resources, his lack of an heir with her youth and attractiveness, his dilatory paralysis with her initiative and energy, her neediness with his ability to navigate the legal niceties in her favour.

There's no need to be sentimental about Ruth's story. She faces a terrible crisis as the story begins. It's not necessary to portray her simply as a pious, devoted daughter-in-law who discovers an influential kinsman and patron, and makes him her husband. She uses guile and seduction to achieve what her lowly social status would never have given her. But we also have to recognize what she gives up. In becoming an Israelite, taking on her mother-in-law's family, language, town and religion, she takes the path of total assimilation. If we think about migrants today, host cultures shouldn't be pious and assume that all asylum seekers will be guileless and innocent; but neither may a host culture assert its customs so strongly that it demands every migrant adopts those traditions from the word go.

But just as much as we shouldn't overplay Ruth as a model of the perfect asylum seeker, so we mustn't miss the depth of her story. She sticks with Naomi through thick and thin. Boaz shapes his life to redeem her, and in doing so finds a blessing. Together Ruth and Boaz portray for us the faithfulness of God. This is how God works, with steadfast love, at personal cost, facing adversity, never letting us go, sometimes using guile, sometimes shrewdness, always disarming us with goodness and constantly pointing to a purpose beyond what we can yet see. Ruth is Jesus, who goes into the far country and becomes one like us and brings about our salvation; but Boaz is also Jesus, for, like Jesus, Boaz takes on his shoulders the troubles of one he doesn't need to help and brings deliverance at great cost to himself.

Now this brings us to the central point. The issue of immigration is conventionally discussed as a question of duty. The issue is whether Britain is obliged to take in people who are fleeing persecution elsewhere, how one can verify that the claim is genuine, whether one has to limit the number even of the persecuted, and whether anyone migrating largely for economic benefit has any right to be here. What Ruth's story shows is that the foreigner who appears to be nothing more than a bundle of trouble turns out to bring vital initiative and energy, and ultimately becomes the harbinger of the nation's hope of renewal. And what Ruth evokes in the host country is to stir in Boaz an awareness of his own scarcity and to inspire him to actions that write his place in salvation history. To turn our back on migrants is to forget our identity, inhibit our renewal and deny our destiny.

I'm not saying we should take away border controls and dismantle quota policies. But I am saying it's time to change our framework for this whole conversation. Migrants are not fundamentally a threat and a danger. They are first and foremost a challenge to the Church to reinhabit its true identity and a gift to the nation to rediscover its lost energy. You can have too much of a good thing: but immigrants are fundamentally a good thing. We're all migrants, or the sons and daughters thereof; Jesus was a migrant too. To forget that is to forget who we are and to forget who God is.

And the reason I have a particular care for this issue is that I am a migrant. I was born in Canada, was brought to the UK as a baby, and as an adult I left to make a life in the USA. I migrated back to the UK a few years ago. On each occasion I was welcomed as a stranger and seen as a blessing, a source of hope and renewal. And most importantly, in 1938 my mother came to this country as an asylum seeker. The danger she escaped was real: she left Berlin just in time. She learnt a new language and new customs in a foreign land. In time she found her Boaz. And that's how I came to be here today. I can't avoid the conclusion that if Britain had had the same attitude and policy towards asylum seekers then that it has today, I would never have been born.

And, by the way, I didn't mention my mother's name. She was called Ruth.

Notes

1 See Jonathan Sacks, *The Dignity of Difference: How to Avoid the Clash of Civilizations* (London: Continuum, 2004), p. 58.
2 For the idea of citing Ruth and for much of what follows, I am grateful to Susannah Snyder, *Asylum-Seeking, Migration and Church* (London: Ashgate, 2012).

1

The ethics of global relationships

Rowan Williams

'Who is my neighbour?' said the lawyer to Jesus. Why didn't Jesus give him a clearer answer? Why didn't he simply say 'everybody', and leave it at that? The story of the Good Samaritan, which Jesus tells in response to that question, is a story not just about who we're supposed to love – it's a story about how we become lovable; it's a story about how we move from the passive to the active; it's a story about how we recognize our life as bound up with the act and being of a stranger. In other words, it's a story that operates at several levels, and leaves us with a huge amount to think over.

Who is my neighbour? Jesus turns the question back, eventually, and asks the lawyer, 'Who was a neighbour to the man who fell among the thieves?' The neighbour, in other words, is not somebody sitting over there passively waiting for me to be good to them. The neighbour is me already involved in the life of another, already moving towards someone else, not passive, but active. So part of Jesus' answer to the lawyer's question is that we are invited *to define ourselves as neighbours.* The lawyer would like to think of a world where you knew who neighbours were and who neighbours weren't; ideally, a world where you could be reasonably sure that when you loved a certain number of people as much as you could, that would be all right, and the rest could look after themselves. By moving all of this into the realm of action and choice, Jesus in effect says to us, 'It's not a matter of deciding who out there deserves to be loved by you; it's a question of your decision to *be* a neighbour – your decision to be someone who offers life to the "other".'

The Samaritan in the story is a neighbour because he saves life. Can we then decide to be neighbours by deciding to save life? This surely is one of the important questions that the Good Samaritan story puts back to us in the name of Jesus, moving us, as I said, into an active rather than a passive mode. We have to decide something; we are not told how to catalogue the list of people we are obliged to love, but invited to make a basic change which turns our lives into life-giving realities.

The Samaritan is a neighbour because the man on the Jericho road owes him his life. And we are most deeply neighbours to one another, and to and in our world, when there are others who owe us life; and we recognize them as neighbours because we know we owe *them* life. So to love a neighbour is to love the person who can save your life. And of course the extra catch in the story of the Good Samaritan is that since you never quite know who that is, and since it's likely to be the most improbable person around, your openness to neighbourliness has to be a profound, all-encompassing, all-embracing affair.

This apparently simple story about the Good Samaritan leaves us, as do all of Jesus' great parables, with a question about who we are, where we put ourselves in the story; and, like all Jesus' great parables, it leaves us with an uneasy sense that we could be any of the characters in the story, or indeed all of them at various points. That's to say, we are the people who find admirable and sometimes religious excuses for not doing what we ought; we are the people who are left helpless at the side of the road by a violent and meaningless world; and we are, at least potentially, the people who decide to give life.

So 'the ethics of global relationships' – a resonantly abstract title, worthy of a Cambridge academic – is not about how to construct a system of universal morality. It's first and foremost recognizing a summons to be life-givers, to be to others the surprising strangers who bring them alive; and one of the implications of that is that we must expect to be brought alive by surprising strangers. As Jesus' story also suggests, a great deal of our habitual life ignores this. We imagine that life is simply something we've got, and which ideally we're not obliged to share. We shall be able to find many reasons for retaining our suspicion of the stranger. We may even, like the priest and the Levite in the story, find a way of treating the obvious neighbour – the fellow Jew by the side of the road – as a stranger.

Part of the force of the parable is that in Jesus' time the three classifications of God's people were priests, Levites and Israelites; there they all are in the story, and the priest and the Levite don't want to recognize the Israelite whom they treat as a stranger – perhaps a polluting dead body, perhaps some embarrassing presence who will be a drag on them, their purity and their security. In the light of this, we are reminded that global relationship is no bland matter: not a question of universal benevolence, not a question of saying the whole world is my friend. It is anchored in a very particular encounter; it may be a discovery of our obligation to a familiar 'neighbourly' figure that we have got into the habit of ignoring, or a discovery of the immediacy and familiarity of someone who has nothing apparently in common with us. In either case, global relationship means the willingness to be a surprising stranger and to be surprised by strangers, and in that, to let neighbourliness come alive.

Dietrich Bonhoeffer, in the years leading up to the Second World War, was beginning to work on Christian ethics, and we still have the drafts that he prepared for a major book on the subject before he was imprisoned by the Nazi regime and finally executed. Bonhoeffer's work on ethics is an attempt to turn on its head quite a lot of the ways in which Christians are used to doing ethics; and he does it by saying that Christian ethics is essentially about standing where Jesus stands and taking responsibility with him for representing the world. That's where ethics begins: in the decision to speak on behalf of, to stand in for, and stand with any and every human situation.

Now of course, says Bonhoeffer, this doesn't mean that each of us carries an infinite responsibility. We're not, as a matter of fact, God. But each one of us carries a responsibility that is going to come alive in ways we cannot predict. And one of the things that Bonhoeffer says most emphatically and clearly, in the surviving fragments of what would have been an extraordinary book on ethics, is that our greatest mistake is to try to spell out in advance who we're responsible for – in other words, to try to answer the question 'Who is my neighbour?' neatly and conclusively so that we don't have to be bothered by the people we hadn't planned for. For Bonhoeffer, universal responsibility is a matter of readiness *moment by moment* to stand in for and to stand with whatever human neighbour is around; and that, says Bonhoeffer, is the heart of the being and the logic of the Church. The Church does as a matter of fact, he says, take up a bit of room in the world – you can't just be an invisible church. Sooner or later people will spot it. But the space the Church takes up in the world, he says, is the space that it holds and occupies on behalf of everybody. That's to say, the Church is not there to defend its territory – here's the religious bit, or the Christian bit, here's the ethical bit; no, the Church occupies space so as to say, 'We will guarantee this for everyone; we will keep open here the promise of a solidarity without any advance restriction.' And it's in this way, according to Bonhoeffer, that the Church shows what and who Jesus is. For him, the theology of global relationship began with a recognition that in Jesus Christ, God stands in for and stands with any and every human person – that's what the life of Jesus and the death of Jesus are all about. If we are to live with him, in his neighbourhood, in his Spirit, in his power, that's where we stand and that's what we seek to realize.

So if Bonhoeffer is right, and if my hearing of Jesus' parable is right, the ethics of global relationship is an ethic that has to do with creating relationship. It is about the decision, wherever we are, in whatever human situation, to make a bond, to stand with and, as Bonhoeffer says – and it's a challenging phrase – potentially to stand in for the 'other'; that is, to take what's coming to them, to shoulder their burden on their behalf. It is about creating relationships that rest upon a recognition that no one of us is who he or she is alone, no one of us exists in a vacuum or as an atom, no one of us comes into being full grown, self-sufficient. Our human life is constantly receiving who we are from those around us and in turn giving our life that they may be alive.

It may sound very advanced, and spiritual, and even mystical, but it's the basic fact of our language, our interaction, the gestures by which parent and child communicate. That's where it all begins: we begin to be who we are because we are related. And of course, in our human lives, we're related always and already in ways we never chose, and never planned. We are embarrassingly bound up with the life of everybody else around us. We'd much rather not be – it'd be good if we could trace our pedigree to some independent source, not infected by the embarrassing failures of the human race at large, just as we'd all like in the Church to be independent of the failures of the Church at large.

But we're bound in already. And when we decide to be a neighbour, when we decide to embark on a style of life that gives life, we're not in fact just doing something in a vacuum; we are recognizing and acting out the truth that is deepest in us, the fact of interdependence. When I decide to be a neighbour, and when I decide to be the one who gives life, I decide to be what I most deeply am – I recognize and enter into that deep exchange by which human beings constantly make one another human. So to speak of the ethics of creating relationship is not to speak of a decision to be good or to be nice against the odds. It's to speak of a decision to be what we are, which carries with it a recognition that when we don't give life, and when we do create, not neighbours, but strangers and enemies, we're actually doing something unnatural.

It's one of the great and important teachings of classical theology that evil is unnatural. That's to say, we as human beings are not instinctively at home with hostility, fear and violence. And the Church has affirmed that in the teeth of most of the evidence for most of its history. As some theologians have said, it actually takes a lot of effort to be wicked. When Jesus says to St Paul in the Acts of the Apostles, 'It hurts you to kick against the goads' (Acts 26.14), he's saying something very like this. It is actually a great and unnecessary investment of energy and ingenuity to create enemies and strangers rather than neighbours. It's not what we are made for.

And while it's certainly no part of the Church's job to pretend that people are better and nicer than they are, it is a crucial part of the Church's job to say that the natural, the homely, the obvious for the human race is neighbourhood, not suspicion. So that when we struggle to be neighbours and to encourage others to be neighbours, we're not inviting human beings to go against the grain, to make some great act of defiance in the face of an unjust and hostile fate. We are saying that the deepest condition of our humanity is recognition, interaction and the exchange of life. That in turn implies that when I identify somebody else as a stranger, an enemy, I am alienating some part of myself – I am making something of myself a stranger, and an enemy; I am losing something of who I am.

So the ethics of global relationship is a matter first of all of discovering the courage to have faith in a universal and given human solidarity, an involvement with one another that is already there in virtue of God's creative gift of life to us as a human community, not only as individuals; and then to have the courage to behave as if that were true, to love the stranger as the one who could save your life.

To love the stranger as the one who could save your life: many years ago, I was visiting an urban parish in Coventry, and after the Sunday morning service got into conversation with an elderly lady from the parish who was surrounded by a family of obviously Caribbean origin. The two little girls in this family were clinging on to the old lady's arms and jumping up and down with great enthusiasm, and she was obviously completely devoted to them.

She told me that not very long before, when the children had been even smaller, the family had moved in next door to her. She'd been profoundly suspicious of them. She came from a generation where black neighbours were thought of as threatening. The children would occasionally knock on her door, or peer through her window. She was very annoyed about this because she thought they were intruding into her private space, until one day she had an accident in the house, and was left sprawled on the floor of her front room. The children from next door, looking through the window, saw her and called an ambulance. 'The stranger as the one who could save your life' couldn't be more vivid than it was in that little encounter; and I remember her saying with tears in her eyes, 'I can't do enough for them now.' She had discovered her own life-giving freedom because she discovered a stranger who could save her life.

All of this is fleshed out at length and in depth in some of St Paul's writings. That picture of ourselves being diminished by the diminishing of another, of every member of the body suffering because another suffers or rejoicing because another rejoices – that is at the very heart of the idea of the Church. Everything else about the Church depends on this. I can't say that too emphatically. Everything about the Church depends upon this – this being involved with one another, beyond our choice and our preference, to the extent that we are less ourselves when we turn the other away, and more ourselves when we become neighbours. It's also about something further and quite demanding, which I think could be best expressed by saying that this implies a kind of *attention* to where we are; a kind of close, realistic, patient and loving absorption of the specifics of where we are. Because, going back to what I was saying earlier, the point is not that we should suddenly develop generalized niceness, but that we should discover and act out what it might be to give life *here*, in this moment, in this relationship. And if that's to be the case, we need to have our eyes and ears and hearts keenly attuned to where there is death in our situation – if we are to give life, we need to know what kinds of death are around, what are the needs to which we are actually responding.

We all know, I suspect with painful clarity, what it's like to try to give someone the help they don't need. Many people spend their entire lives doing this, and there are a certain number of institutions devoted to doing it as well; and we're all familiar also with the old chestnut 'I'm a great lover of humanity; it's just the people I can't stand'. In contrast to that, a true ethic of global relationship begins from a very keen and clear sense of the local and specific. It's not that 'charity begins at home' in the rather unhelpful sense that phrase increasingly attracts to itself. It's simply that unless we are prepared selflessly to attend to what is in front of our noses, to know the difference between real and fictional need, to know the actual three-dimensional reality of the 'other', then we're not going to be of any use to anyone. And however loudly, however passionately, we speak of 'global ethics', we shall have missed something all-important by ignoring the immediate.

Earlier on I quoted Bonhoeffer on how universal responsibility is not a matter of trying to be responsible for everybody. It is having eyes and heart open enough to see in situation after situation where the specific need and hunger for life is; to attend lovingly in that way so we are able to give life where it's needed, and also to *receive* it, where there is death within us. Now to speak of life and death in this way and to speak of neighbourliness in this context is in our own age an issue that has taken on an extra dimension. If we're on the lookout for those areas and aspects of human life where death is at work, if we're on the lookout for where life is truly needed, we're bound to be looking at our environment with an eye that says, 'What in our entire context gives or denies life?' Which is why this entire approach to the ethics of neighbourliness requires us to look not just at our human environment, but at that wider environment that makes us alive. Increasingly scholars and thinkers have been writing about the need for us to rediscover the environment itself as a 'neighbour'. That is to say, we live in a world whose strangeness makes us alive, and so we live in a world that we must not be hostile to, a world we must not regard as our enemy, a world we must give life to as it gives life to us.

It's very hard to deny that, in our current cultural context, the works of death are very visible in a degraded and threatened environment, and the need is urgent for people of faith and no particular faith to recover a sense that the material environment itself is a neighbour, and to be loved in a neighbourly way. If we are resolved to be neighbours without any condition, and if we know that environmental damage and degradation takes away life from the human neighbour, we need to change our behaviours; we need once again to decide to be neighbours to our neighbourhood, our physical, material neighbourhood; we need a neighbourly vision of the material world, the animal world, the inanimate world. That's to say that there's no global ethics without an ethic of the globe, the actual globe we inhabit. Because the environmental neighbour is the world in which my life lives, and the world in which my use of that environment can enhance or deny life in another.

Who is my neighbour? My neighbour is the stranger who gives me life. My neighbour therefore is the stranger to whom I must give life, because my life and theirs are already bound up together. The reality of the Church is a reality rooted in the recognition of this mutual implication of life and life. The Church is supposed to be a place where this unlimited neighbourly decision can be nourished and re-inforced day by day in our neighbourly practices within the community – our building up of one another, our giving life to one another. And it's probably a very simple and overly naive thing to say about the Church, yet it does seem that one of the questions we ought to be asking more often than we do, in our often bitter controversies in the Church, is whether we are giving life to our Christian neighbour in any important or interesting sense, or dealing death.

And all of that is what I mean by saying that I don't believe global ethics is a universal system of behaviour. It's not even a matter of trying to find 'common values' across different world-views. There are those who write very eloquently about global ethics as a search for those values that Christians and Muslims and Hindus and humanists all hold in common. That's all very well, but I suspect that it doesn't move us very much further forward in understanding what action we have to take in order to be global neighbours, those actions of giving life. In contrast, Jesus' story of the Good Samaritan asks each of us whether and how we hold back our willingness to be a neighbour, inviting us to examine the various rationales we might give for not giving life. And no amount of discourse about shared values will quite get us to that point, because no amount of theoretical discussion of ethics will quite get us to the point of repentance and conversion – the clear recognition of what there is of death in us; the clear commitment to allowing life to come into us and to be shared with others.

The Christian gospel declares that holding back our willingness to be a neighbour is quite close to the essence of alienation from who and what we are. As I said earlier, the more strangers and enemies we make, the more likely we are to be strangers and enemies to something in ourselves. And that (to underline the point again) is not simply a recommendation for blandness, unquestioning acceptance and universal niceness. It's the call to honesty, to a keen awareness of how very easily I can fracture and alienate myself, and to honesty about the levels of fracture and alienation in others.

To give life to the neighbour, to see the neighbour as the stranger who can save your life, doesn't mean that we must nurture illusions that other people are nicer than they really are; it doesn't solve all at once how we actually negotiate real and deep conflicts. This is long and hard work, and there is no quick formula that will get us through it. The point is simply to turn the question back, again and again, to our own hearts. How are we alienated from ourselves? How are we strangers to ourselves? How do we become natural? How do we come home?

A great Roman Catholic theologian, the Dominican Herbert McCabe, used to say that ethics was all about doing what you wanted to do; the problem was that most of us had absolutely no idea what we truly wanted most of the time. To become 'natural' is hard work, and I've often found myself saying that the advice 'just be yourself', given to somebody else, is arguably the most unhelpful piece of advice in the world. (As if we could!) But the Christian gospel, and the theology that arises from it, says that the deep, un-alienated self, who we really are, is, first of all, already connected, already interdependent, already involved; and second, we can be set free to bring it to the surface, to act it out and show it to be true – we can be reconnected with who we are to become ourselves; and we can act so as to show who we are, who Christ is (if we're Christians), who God is. Rejection of the stranger, abuse of the environment, systemic suspicion, war and injustice, show not what we are but what we're deeply not. They show the ways in which (as I said earlier) we can with ingenuity, and effort, and energy, constantly kick against the goads, and deny the humanity we share.

There is always, therefore, a likelihood that the appeal to global relationship will not be universally popular. We know our capacity of turning away from the truth and turning away from ourselves – we know sin. And there it continues to sit in our hearts. And yet for all such tragic moments when we recognize the damage we can do ourselves, something remains in us still capable of coming alive in connection, still capable of neighbourliness. Our identity as neighbours obstinately surfaces again and again. When the media tell us how deeply threatened we are by hordes of strangers on our shores, mysteriously a remarkable number of people still shed tears over the sufferings of refugees and put themselves out to support them, even while, if you asked many of them, they would say they believed what is in the media. We are, thank God, deeply inconsistent and confused beings.

And that, in conclusion, oddly enough, is a foundation for thinking about global ethics and global responsibility. We need to be reminded (and we are constantly) of how very easily we slip into those attitudes of estranging the 'other'. We need to be reminded how deep that goes in us. We need, of course, practically, again and again, to find our way through genuine conflict, genuine rivalry and competition. And yet people undertake these tasks, people respond almost without thinking to the call to be neighbourly, as if they recognize some truth in it.

The Christian faith affirms that we are already connected profoundly and ineradicably to one another. It tells us that we forget this, constantly, daily; and also that our forgetfulness is not final. We can be restored to who we are – we can remember ourselves. And to take that other great parable in St Luke's Gospel, you may remember that the turning point for the prodigal son was when he 'came to himself' and recognized that he had been running away from dependence and involvement and relationship, gratitude and gift, and returned to surprise his family – certainly his elder brother, and doubtless his father as well – and to be surprised in turn by the immediate life-giving response that met him.

Who is my neighbour? The stranger who will save my life. Who am I? A life-giving stranger for someone else. 'Go,' says Jesus, 'and do that.' Don't leave it at the level of a theoretical question – 'Can I make a list of people to whom I am indebted?' – because you will never finish with that task, and it misconceives it anyway. You're not trying to discharge a debt of love that you owe to others. You are simply there to be the one who stands with, stands in for, occupies space for, the stranger. You are there to be a channel of life. And as some theologians of our own age have said, when we think about ethics, it's often important to liberate ourselves just from thinking about good and evil, and to start thinking instead about life and death. And when Jesus tells the lawyer to go and do likewise, essentially he tells him, and us, to go and be alive, to go and make alive.

2

Politics as a form of neighbour love

Luke Bretherton

I want to suggest that politics is not merely an arena for practising neighbour love but can of itself be a form of neighbour love. However, this is only possible when a Christian conception of neighbour love, one born out of the life, death and resurrection of Jesus Christ, reconfigures how core political relations are understood. To substantiate these claims, let me begin by defining the term 'politics'.

Politics is both a substantive good and a practice. Politics as a good refers to the shared, common, or public life of the polity as a whole. Other terms for this common life include the commonwealth, commonweal, or *res publica*. The good that inheres in the form and structure of the polity as a whole is that of *politea*: the good of political association or common life and the structures and processes that enable this good to be tilled and tended. As a good, association is both a substantive end to be pursued in itself and a means through which to fulfil other kinds of substantive goods (such as health and education). As a good, politics is directed to the flourishing of the whole rather than the part, the common rather than either factional or private interest.

Politics is not just an end, it is a practice. The good of association entails both the formal means and structures for ordering a common life and also the relational practices through which a common world of meaning and action is cultivated. Thus, the term 'politics' also refers to the craft of politics understood as the formation and negotiation of a common life between friends and strangers and their estranged or competing interests and visions of the good. Or, to put it another way, politics is the craft through which to maintain commonality and recognize and conciliate conflict with others in pursuit of goods in common and a shared vision of human flourishing.

Politics in this second sense requires a set of practices through which to recognize and maintain commonality and conciliate conflict. Politics as a set of practices or craft takes place in multiple settings and is not co-extensive with control of the state or even dependent on there being a state. And it is certainly not to be reduced to party politics. Nomads in the desert, who live outside of any formal state structures, generate a rich form of political life through customary practices of hospitality and greeting, for example, through which a common life based on shared goods (such as access to water) is sustained over time. Elders and pastors in a church negotiating service times are practising the craft of politics.

Politics as a craft for building relationships and making judgements about what is common entails acting in a way appropriate to the time/*kairos*, hence the need for judgements about what is best for these people, in this place, at this time (how, when and where should we act and what should we do?). As action in time, politics involves questions of power (how to act, who does what to whom, and how we achieve our goals). This in turn raises questions about legitimacy (why should we act this way rather than that way, who gets to act, and what is the meaning and purpose of our actions?) and what I call wily wisdom (the local knowledge, strategic analysis and practical skills necessary to respond appropriately to a constantly changing and ambiguous environment).

Politics in both the senses outlined here is categorically not war by other means. To be at war or engage in armed revolt (whether just or not) is to move into a qualitatively different kind of human interaction – one that signals the end of politics and the start of something else. The 'bullet' and the 'ballot box' are mutually exclusive routes to solving shared problems. At a basic level, politics is the alternative to physical violence and cycles of revenge. Consequently, politics should not be used as a synonym for talk of power understood as a negative and wholly violent phenomenon. The primary focus of politics is relational power (power with), not unilateral, command and control forms of power (power over). Building relational power demands listening to and negotiating with others rather than forcing them to do what you want by means of violent coercion or some oppressive system. A commitment to politics grounded on relational power thereby entails a tacit commitment to non-violence as a better form of human interaction, a commitment made explicit and developed in philosophical, spiritual and tactical ways in a wide range of political movements. Examples include the anti-imperial Indian movement struggling for independence from Great Britain, the American civil rights movement, the United Farm Workers movement in California, the 'Velvet Revolution', which overthrew Communism in

Czechoslovakia, 'People's Power', which ended the Marcos dictatorship in the Philippines, and Mass Action for Peace by Christian and Muslim women in Liberia, which helped end the recent civil war there.

For politics to be possible, those engaged in it must assume that not everyone is or should be the same, but that a common world of meaning and action is achievable despite differences. Politics, as a tacitly non-violent form of inter- action, entails a commitment to conditions in which worlds of shared meaning and action can be created or sustained. By contrast, violence represents the destruction of the institutions, practices and habits through which mutual communication and relationship are made possible. The commitment to discovering some form of shared world of meaning and action displays the basic moral requirement that politics as a good entails a commitment to the dignity of friends and strangers (which includes those we find scan- dalous). Politics thereby involves a vision of a common life that can be sustained and renewed through time and as something more than the aggregation of individual choices. Yet too much moral conviction, combined with a belief in one's own innocence and the absolute rightness of one's cause, inhibits the kinds of negotiations and neighbourly relations necessary to forge a common life between friends and strangers. Moreover, the use of political authority not simply to restrain evil but to enforce virtue is as much of a problem as is its use for corrupt and oppressive ends. Terror and totalitarianism are as often born of a zeal for righteous- ness as of a desire to dominate. All that being said, and despite being a penultimate good and the alternative to interpersonal violence and war, in a fallen world, politics is inherently caught up in forging and sustaining idolatrous structures of domination. However, there are distinctly anti-political forms of domination, from which politics should be distinguished.

The first and most obvious kinds of anti-politics are those that consolidate the rule of the one over and against the many. The rule of the one may take the form of one party, despot, dictator, movement or ideology, with any alternative centres of power or forms of life being viewed as a threat to the sovereign rule of the one. Totalitarianism, authoritarianism and other kinds of tyrannous, unjust, unaccountable and arbitrary rule are the manifestation of this form of anti-politics. Examples include the Soviet Union, Nazi Germany and Western colonial forms of rule.

The second kind of unilateral anti-politics is technocracy, which is constituted by the rule of the few over and against the many. It grows out of various attempts to overcome the need for learning and practising the craft of politics – and the contingency, uncertainty and lack of control politics entails – through different forms of legal, bureaucratic and market-based procedures. Technocracy is often posed as the alternative to and remedy for tyranny. It is not. Rather, technocratic regimes attempt to close down or corrode various 'informal' – that is, non-state – forms of political life, thereby undermining the ability of ordinary persons to learn the craft of politics. This paradoxically anti-political form of 'politics' is about following a bureaucratic procedure, conformity to regulations, or the application of an economic 'law', regardless of whether these do or do not contribute to building up a just and generous common life.

Massive amounts of human suffering can result from demanding conformity to the procedure, policy or law, but this is either ignored or seen as collateral damage necessary to make the system (whether administrative, legal or economic) work efficiently and effectively. For the political theorist Hannah Arendt, a pointed example of exactly this dynamic was the Nazi Adolf Eichmann, who refused to exercise judgement in the name of conforming to legal and bureaucratic regulations and so aided and abetted the Holocaust. As this illustrates, technocracy can be aligned with tyranny, particularly in its totalitarian forms.

Another example is the effect of capitalism on working conditions, impoverishing and degrading millions of people, justifying this by reference to the 'laws' of economics. Ignoring the human and ecological cost of following a procedure is not accidental. What the sociologist Max Weber called the 'iron cage' of bureaucratic, legal and economic calculation and control is a deliberate attempt to separate moral questions from political and economic ones in the name of creating a more rational and well-ordered social and political life. Within this technocratic framework, morality and religious beliefs and practices are understood as private and personal, while political life and economic life are seen as public, 'neutral', disenchanted, reasonable and amoral. The iron cage is one of the dominant frameworks within which politics is imagined today. A theological understanding of politics must refuse this separation and understand that political and economic judgements are always already moral judgements, and political life is inherently sacred and secular. Imagining politics through the lens of the iron cage is the primary framework used in the fields of economics and political science, and it generates a top-down, anti-political vision of politics much given to careless experiments in social engineering.

Alongside tyranny and technocracy, we must attend to how politics, even at its best, can generate forms of domination. Here the problem can be framed as the rule of the many over and against either the few or the one who is perceived as 'other'. To understand this dynamic in the contemporary context, it is helpful to see how it operated in the Greco-Roman world, where many key Western political concepts and terms originated. In that ancient context, authentic politics could only take place within a city/*polis*. The *polis* was the basis of a 'civilized' common life. But not everyone involved in the cultivation of this civilized common life was considered equal. One grouping – women, slaves and children – was confined to the *oikos* or household, understood as a private sphere that was segregated from the arena of politics. Another group was composed of foreigners, who were not considered part of the common life of the city. Both those confined to the *oikos* and those perceived as external to the *polis* were judged as being incapable and unworthy of enjoying the good/moral life, so were excluded from practising the craft of politics. Only property-owning men were capable of a truly flourishing life and so only they were qualified to participate in political life, which was the primary and most significant arena of human fulfilment.

To clarify my point about how politics can generate forms of domination I will focus on the status of the foreigner/barbarian in this classical framework, as this has analogies with how we still view non-citizens as uncivilized and subject to suspicion. It will also make clear how neighbour love reconfigures and resignifies the account of politics given so far.

Those judged to be outsiders/non-citizens, whether resident within the boundaries of the city or living elsewhere, were potential if not actual enemies, whose way of life threatened the very existence of the city, and the city was the condition and possibility of the well-being of its citizens. The physical, moral and spiritual flourishing of the individual citizen was coterminous with the flourishing of the city and vice versa. Other, alien forms of life, not identified as sharing in and contributing to the flourishing of the city, were necessarily either potentially seditious (if they were resident aliens) or a threat (if they were foreign). Alien forms of life had to be guarded against, and if they disturbed the peace they had to be either repressed (if inside the walls) or repelled (if outside). Internal and external 'others' were also a means by which the common life of 'our' city came to be defined and understood. 'We, the people' are not like 'them', and all that the other is imagined to be (effeminate, uncivilized, treacherous, cruel) is all that 'we' are not (virile, loyal, brave, honest, rational).

The influential German jurist and one-time Nazi Carl Schmitt made a virtue of friend–enemy relations, seeing them as the basis of political life. He criticized modern liberal democracies for failing to take friend–enemy relations seriously, and thereby being anti-political. Given the fallen character of earthly political life, Schmitt is not wholly wrong. Throughout history, civilizations have imagined themselves opposed to various internal and external others, and friend–enemy relations are deeply constitutive of the nature and form of political life. This is no less true of Western streams of Christianity than it is of city states like Athens, empires like the Roman, Ottoman or Ming, or atheistic states like the former Soviet Union. Jews have been the primary internal 'other', while Muslims and non-whites have been the external others against whom a Western European and confessionally Christian civilization has imagined itself. This self-understanding has thereby justified the repression or subjugation of Jews and Muslims, and then non-white peoples.

This repression and subjugation echoes the tendency of all earthly political orders to absolutize friend–enemy distinctions and see in such distinctions points of moral and spiritual difference. For example, when white people are seen as purer and of greater worth than black people, this in turn justifies the oppression of black people and their exclusion from citizenship. Theologically, friend–enemy relations are relativized but not superseded, at least not until Jesus returns. The universal scope of God's love and presence calls into question any attempt to absolutize friend–enemy relations. The heretic Samaritan and the pagan Syrophoenician woman, no less than the faithful Jewish man, can teach us something about God, about how to live well and how God can be present in 'their' form of life, despite that being very different from 'ours'. The New Testament echoes a deep logic of the Hebrew Scriptures. It is Tamar (Genesis 38) and Ruth who are the forebears of David. Two marginal and acutely vulnerable figures (childless widows) from peoples despised by the Israelites – the Canaanites and the Moabites – are nevertheless paradigms of faithfulness. And before Tamar and Ruth, it is Rahab, a marginal and vulnerable woman of questionable status (a prostitute) from an avowed enemy, not any male Israelite spy, who is the first person to recognize what God is doing in the promised land and respond faithfully (Joshua 1—2). Enemies and those we find scandalous can know better who God is, and can teach those self-identified as the people of God what it means to be faithful, loving and just.

This is not to say that Christians do not have a distinctive vision of the good life that others can threaten and undermine, but it should prohibit any attempt to absolutize distinctions between Christians and non-Christians or interpret them through the grid of friend–enemy relations. Friend–enemy relations are fallen rather than created, but can be redeemed. As fellow creatures made in the image of God, who are fallen and finite humans, non-Christian others participate with Christians in a common, penultimate, earthly world in which God is nevertheless active and present. If politics is simply a contingent, this-worldly, 'secular' endeavour that is nevertheless located within a cosmos that has meaning and purpose, then I can relinquish control, trusting that the other and I exist in a common world of meaning and action. I can thereby compromise without compromising the end of history. As a fallen and finite human who participates with others in a penultimate yet common world of meaning and action, I can trust that the other may well have something to teach me about how to live well, and even if I profoundly disagree with him or her, a common life is still possible.

The scriptural demand to listen to and learn from others should prohibit Christians from turning conflicts concerning material resources (oil, water, land) and penultimate goods (education, health) into ultimate, Manichean conflicts of good against evil, thereby rejecting the possibility of a common life in the face of disagreement. When Christians do this, it is because they are overinvested in worldly projects of salvation, having lost sight of the ultimate and made a god of the penultimate. The theological term for this kind of overinvestment is idolatry, and it is unequivocally condemned as sinful. Moreover, the crucified Jesus shatters all attempts to stabilize any one way of life as the basis of true humanity to which all others should conform. Everyone needs conversion, and the Church is always in need of reformation. Conversely, building a common life with strangers and enemies is a profound act of faith that all things are created in Christ and all things will be reconciled through Christ.

The constructive way in which to frame relations with others is to love one's neighbour. Love of neighbour should disrupt how friend–enemy relations are imagined and constructed, and extend who is included in political life. One way of conceptualizing this, which largely draws inspiration from the work of Aristotle, is understanding politics as a means of generating public friendship. But unlike being a friend, being a neighbour is a vocation that does not depend on liking, having a rapport with, or being equal to others. Neither is it a condition or state of being or pre-assigned role. We discover who our neighbour is within contingent and contextual relationships. Unlike such things as family, class, ethnicity or gender, I cannot predetermine who is my neighbour. Neighbours have neither assigned social identities (such as father, sister) nor institutionally constructed roles (doctor, police officer). On occasion the call of the neighbour supersedes prior commitments and loyalties, whether professional, religious, social or political, and we can encounter a neighbour in any one of our roles. Politics, as a craft through which relations with others can be created and sustained, despite difference and conflicts of interest, is a mode of neighbouring.

Folded into love of neighbour is the call to love our enemies. But Christian 'enemy love' tends to fall into one of three traps. Either we make everyone an enemy (the sectarian temptation to denounce anyone who is not like 'us'), or we make no one an enemy, denying any substantive conflicts and pretending that if we just read our Bibles and pray, things like racism and economic inequality will get better by means of some invisible hand (the temptation of senti-mentalism that denies we are the hands and feet of the body of Christ), or we fail to see how enemies claim to be our friend (the temptation of naivety that ignores questions of power). In relation to the latter trap, we must recognize that the powerful mostly refuse to acknowledge that they are enemies to the oppressed, claiming to be friends to everyone. A loving act in relation to those in power who refuse to acknowledge their oppressive action would be to force those who claim to be friends to everyone (and are thereby friends to no one) to recognize that their actions perpetuate injust-ice and domination, and need renouncing. This involves struggle, culminating in an ongoing dance of conflict and conciliation. Too much conflict and we cannot hear each other, and political debate dissolves into sloganeering, denunciation and eventually violent strife. Too much con-ciliation and we paper over real points of disagreement and foreshorten the debate, thereby failing to discover the truth of the matter and the truth about ourselves. And, like any good dance, politics as a form of neighbour love requires learning certain moves, cultivating certain kinds of disposition and habit (patience, courage, for example), and being able to live with tension. But this dance of conflict and conciliation means that we must learn to see enemies as neighbours capable of change, and recognize that we ourselves must move and change. Agitational democratic politics can be a means through which an active relationship with enemies can be built in order to 'seek the welfare of the city' (Jeremiah 29.7) so that it displays something of what a just and generous common life might look like.

Building any form of just, generous and more neighbourly common life through a dance of conflict and conciliation entails reckoning with a hard truth: everyone must change, and in the process we must all lose something to someone at some point. This is part of what it means to live as frail, finite and fallen creatures. Loss, compromise and negotiation are inevitable if the reconfiguration necessary so that all may flourish is to take place. The temptation and sin of the privileged and powerful is to fix the system so that they lose nothing while others always lose, no matter how hard they work. The fight is to ensure that the loss is not borne disproportionately by the poor and marginalized, and this is a key part of what it means to love our neighbour in a way that is faithful to the life, death and resurrection of Jesus Christ.

Politics as a form of neighbour love does not end at the border of the state and is not restricted to citizens of the same state. Anyone anywhere is a potential neighbour to be loved, and a person's status as a creature of God and neighbour

45

for whom Christ died is prior to and transcends the status ascribed to him or her by a nation state. Refugees and the provision of sanctuary are a case in point. As a practice, providing sanctuary to refugees witnesses to the claim that the authority and rule of Christ transcends any earthly political boundary. If Christ is King, then no earthly sovereign or community has the right to utterly exclude or make an exception of anyone from the status of a human being. The Church is to witness to this, and giving sanctuary to refugees is one such means of faithful witness. Yet as love of neighbour, this love is concrete in form and thereby contrasts with the abstract, cosmopolitan vision of an undifferentiated humanity that informs modern conceptions of humanitarianism.

In contrast to a view of politics that is solely about law, unilateral power, elections and the rational administration of scarce resources, understanding politics as the negotiation of a common life between friends and enemies points in a different direction.

In theological terms, humans can only know the truth about God and what it means to be a sane and humane creature through finitude – that is, by risking negotiated historical relations with others (including non-human others). Through participation in the world around us, humans may discover and then make sense of who we are in relation to God and neighbour. For this to occur, it requires attentiveness to and reception of a world we did not make, and negotiation with others we do not control and yet for myriad reasons with whom we must order our social, economic and political relationships.

Attentiveness and reception, characterized by a posture of listening or contemplation, are the precursors of shared speech and action, and thence the coming into being of a common life. The promise of politics is that despite our differences some form of common life can be discovered. But if the process of discovery is to be faithful, hopeful and loving, it entails rendering ourselves vulnerable to others we don't understand, probably don't like and may even find scandalous or threatening. Politics, understood as action in time through which forms of peaceable, just and generous common life are cultivated, is a necessary part of any such process of discovery. However, before Christ's return, the tragic dimensions of social and political life cannot be avoided, and our shared political action often results in failure. Yet faith, hope and love demand that the risk still be taken.

3

My neighbour, President Trump

Stanley Hauerwas

In his beautifully written memoir *The Shepherd's Life: Modern Dispatches from an Ancient Landscape*, James Rebanks helps those like myself who know nothing about sheep to have some sense of what it means to be a shepherd.[1] Rebanks is well prepared to perform this task as he comes from a lineage of shepherds. Rebanks knows sheep and he helps his reader know something of what he knows. For example, I had no idea that there are so many different species of sheep, and that the breeding of sheep can be quite specialized. There are breeds of sheep that have been and continue to be bred to negotiate different topographies.

Romantic conceptions of what it might mean to be a shepherd cannot survive Rebanks' honest account of the brutality that is often necessary to maintain the flock. The bargaining between shepherds can be a cut-throat business. To maintain a farm is sheer hard work and the result is often a barely sustainable living. If you are tempted to become a shepherd you need to remember that you will spend a good deal of your life looking into the mouth of sheep – looking at their teeth seems to tell you much about the quality of a sheep.

Rebanks is a wonderful storyteller and writer. He knows how to write, because although he hated formal schooling he improbably ended up doing a degree at Oxford. He left secondary school as soon as it was permissible, but then discovered that he loved to read. Every night after a hard day of working on the farm belonging to his grandfather and father, he read. While pursuing a continuing education course, he was encouraged to take the tests necessary for him to go to university. He did take the tests and the rest is history.

Having gone to Oxford, he could have pursued a very different form of life from that of being a shepherd, but he chose to return to the farm. He did so because, as he observes, he had inherited from his grandfather the classic world-view of the peasant. That world-view he identified with the presumption that his place was in the line of those people who just always seem to be 'there': people who though often battered yet endure, and through such endurance come to believe that they 'owned the earth'. Such people, Rebanks observes, are 'built out of stories' that are embedded in the everyday necessities of life.

In the last paragraphs of *The Shepherd's Life*, Rebanks, having been a shepherd for many years, describes a moment in his busy life. It is late spring and he is in the process of returning his flock to the craggy hills. These sheep have been bred to fend for themselves in a rocky terrain. He enjoys watching the sheep find their way in the rough fields because they are evidently happy to be 'home'. Rebanks imitates his flock's sense that all is as it should be by lying down in the grass to drink sweet and pure water from the nearby stream. He rolls on his back and watches the clouds racing by. His well-trained sheep dogs, Floss and Tan, who have never seen him so relaxed, come and lie next to him. He breathes in the cool mountain air, he listens to the ewes calling to the lambs to follow them through the rocky crags, and he thinks, 'This is my life. I want no other' (p. 287).

'This is my life. I want no other' is an extraordinary declaration that one rarely hears today.[2] As odd as it may seem, I want to suggest that the loss of our ability to have such lives, the absence of the conditions that make such a declaration possible in contemporary life, is a clue for understanding our current cultural moment and corresponding politics. Stated differently, that many people feel they are forced to live lives they do not want or understand helps explain the phenomenon called Donald Trump. An extraordinary claim; so let me try to explain.

God knows it is hard to take Donald Trump seriously, but I think it is a mistake to ignore him or, more important, to ignore the people that support him. Trump has given voice to an unease that is widespread at this time in our culture. Theories abound about who the people are that support Trump, as well as why they do. I suspect that there is something to most of these theories. I am sure, for example, that racism plays a role for some. It is hard to believe that we had a person running for the presidency of the United States promising to restore law and order. If you ever wanted an exemplification of the oft-made observation that Americans forget their history, note how Trump's claim ignores the racist presumption that gave birth to the phrase 'law and order'.[3] I am also sure that the fear occasioned by September 11 was another factor that attracted some to his declaration to 'make America great again'.

Yet the racism and fear Trump uses to give the impression that he is a 'strong leader' I believe are manifestations of an even deeper pathology: namely, the profound sense of unease that many Americans have about their lives. That unease often takes the form of resentment against elites, but even more troubling, it funds the prejudice against minority groups as well as immigrants. 'Resentment' is another word for the unease that seems to grip many good, middle-class – mostly white – people.[4] These are people who have worked hard all their lives yet find they are no better off than when they started.[5] They deeply resent what they interpret as the special treatment some receive in an effort to right the wrongs of the past.

The bottom line is that many Americans are angry, but they are not sure at whom that anger is appropriately directed. Their anger needs direction and Trump is more than happy to tell Americans, particularly if they are white, who their enemy is, as well as whom they should hate. There is a therapeutic aspect to Trump's rhetoric because he gives people an enemy that delays any acknowledgement that those at whom they should be angry may be themselves.

All this is happening at the same time that the Church, at least the mainstream Church in America, is consumed by a culture of consumption. Americans increasingly discover they have no good reason for going to church. The ever-decreasing number of Christians has led some church leaders to think that our primary job is to find ways to increase church membership. At a time when Christians need to have confidence that we have something to say in the interests of 'church growth', what we have to say is simplistic and superficial. You do not need to come to church to be told you should be nice to those with less.

Of course, that is not the only way the Church has responded to our current political and social challenges. Drawing on the spirit of the civil rights struggle, black and white Christians have again joined with those who seem to represent the progressive forces of history to extend the equality they assume is promised by our democratic convictions. Rightly embarrassed by complicity in past injustices, Christians now try to identify with anyone or any group that claims they want to make America a more just society. Accordingly Christians express their moral commitments by joining with those who think they are having their fundamental rights denied. This is called social ethics. The only problem with this attempt to recover the moral authority of the Church is that while it may be a very good thing for Christians to support these attempts to make our social order more just, it is not theologically clear how the pursuit of justice so understood helps us know how to live. Indeed, I worry that many people now confuse being on the right side of history with having a life worth living.[6]

The Church has simply failed to help people live in a manner such that they would want no other life than the life they have lived. Such lives may well be filled with suffering and failures, but suffering and failures are not blocks to having lived a good life. To have lived a good life is having lived in such a manner that we hope we can be remembered by others – people who have found our lives crucial, making it possible for them to want no other life than the life they have been given. To be happily remembered is to have lived with a modesty that witnesses our dependence on others and makes possible the satisfaction that accompanies doing the right thing without regret or notice.

'This is my life. I want no other' is the expression of what in the past was called 'a good life'. That language is still used but now it references lives that have not been unduly burdened. For many, to have had a good life now means that their second marriage turned out all right, the children did not become addicts, and they had enough savings to retire. That understanding of the good life too often produces people who do not want the life they have lived. They do not want the life they have lived because it is a life without consequence. I suspect the reason why so many men want their service in the military mentioned in their obituary is because they believe that service was of consequence.

If any people should know what it means to have a good life, surely Christians ought to have something to say. Yet I do not think Christians have emphasized sufficiently why we think it so important to have a life well lived, and perhaps even more significant, what living well looks like. I am not, of course, suggesting that what it means to live a good life will be the same for everyone. But I do believe that to have lived well makes it possible to want no other life than the life you have lived. To want no other life than the life we have lived, even with its moments of failure and betrayal, is made possible for Christians because our lives can be located in a determinative narrative that helps us make sense even of those aspects of our life about which we are not sure we can or should make sense.

In his extraordinary book *After Virtue,* first published in 1981, Alasdair MacIntyre observes that the conception of a whole human life is a concept that is no longer generally available in our culture. Such a conception, MacIntyre contends, is necessary to provide the content of non-arbitrary judgements about particular actions or projects that make up our individual lives. The loss of such an understanding of our lives, MacIntyre suggests, has gone unnoticed partly because it is not seen as a loss, but as a gain for human freedom. But the result is the loss of the boundaries derived from our social identity and any sense that our lives are ordered to a given end.[7] Why and how this has happened I want to explore by calling attention to John Milbank and Adrian Pabst's powerful book *The Politics of Virtue: Post-Liberalism and the Human Future.*

The politics of virtue

Milbank and Pabst provide a thick account of the narratives that shape our lives that I think helps explain why so many today cannot be happy with the life they have lived.[8] Milbank and Pabst argue that people who are citizens of advanced societies like the UK and the USA cannot be satisfied with their lives because we no longer have the resources to account for living lives constituted by virtue and honour. As a result we seem to be living lives that are contradictory or, as I suggested above, lives we do not understand.[9]

According to Milbank and Pabst, we are no longer able to live virtuously because our lives are determined by a hegemonic liberal story. That story comes in two basic forms. There is the liberalism of the cultural left, which is primarily understood as the attempt to free people of past forms of oppression. That liberal story is often contrasted with the political and economic liberalism of the right, which is primarily focused on economic and political policy within a capitalist framework. Milbank and Pabst argue, however, that these forms of liberalism, though they have quite different understandings of freedom, have increasingly become mutually reinforcing. The left and the right are joined by the common project to increase personal freedoms even if the result is the atomization of our lives that makes impossible any account of our lives as having a narrative unity. Ironically, societies committed to securing the freedom of the individual end up making that same individual subject to impersonal bureaucratic procedures.

Politically, liberalism increases the concentration of power in the central state, as well as at the same time underwriting the assumption of the inevitability of a globalized market.[10] The latter has the unfortunate effect of destroying a sense of place. In such a social order the production of wealth is increasingly in the hands of a new, rootless oligarchy 'that practises a manipulative populism while holding in contempt the genuine priorities of most people' (p. 1). As good a description of Trump as one could want.

Milbank and Pabst will no doubt be accused, as I often have been when making similar criticisms of liberalism, of failing to provide an adequate account of liberalism – thus the often made observation that characterizations and criticisms of liberalism like Milbank and Pabst's do not take into account the many different forms of liberalism that exist. Nor do those who mount these kinds of criticism of liberalism appropriately acknowledge what has been accomplished through liberalism, such as the freeing of many from arbitrary forms of oppression. I do not think it would be beneficial to pursue these objections given the purpose of this chapter, but suffice it to say that Milbank and Pabst have quite a complex as well as an appreciative understanding of liberalism and acknowledge that liberals have rightly challenged forms of inherited inequalities that both reflect and result in corrupt social arrangements.

I think it will be helpful in support of Milbank and Pabst's account of liberalism to call attention to Ron Beiner's understanding of the subject in his well-regarded book *What's the Matter with Liberalism?*[11] Beiner, perhaps even more forcefully than Milbank and Pabst, stresses that liberalism is not only a social and political alternative but, more important, it is the recommendation of a distinctive moral way to live. To be sure, Milbank and Pabst know that liberalism is a normative proposal for how best to live, but Beiner helps us see that even if we do not think of ourselves as liberals, that story determines our lives. In my language, liberalism is morally the presumption that I am to be held accountable for what I have done only when what I have done is the result of my choice and my choice alone.[12] That is what liberals mean by freedom. As a correlate to this understanding of freedom, equality is understood as the goal of trying to secure for each individual freedom from arbitrary limits.[13]

A liberal way of life, Milbank and Pabst argue, however, is built on contradictory and self-defeating commitments that are only viable because they have been and continue to be parasitic on the heritage past Roman and Christian traditions.

For example, the Christian commitment to the uniqueness of the person conceived and realized through constitutive relations with other persons is lost in the ruthless liberal presumption that our task is to expand our individual domains limited only by contractual agreements made to ensure fairness. The result is an inequity that 'gives rise to endless discontents' that spill over into atavistic assertions of absolute identity of race, nation, religion, gender, sexuality, disability and so on (p. 16).

According to Milbank and Pabst, the contradictory character of liberalism is but an indication that liberalism's most profound mistakes are metaphysical. Liberalism goes against the grain of our humanity and the universe itself. It does so by reducing everything to its bare materiality, which results in a pervasive nihilism. The resulting politics of contractual arrangements, whether it is the politics of Hobbes or of Rousseau, tries to ameliorate the violence that is at the heart of attempts to sustain cooperative relations between isolated individuals. Such arrangements cannot help but fail because a genuine politics cannot be sustained without some account of the role of those who represent what it means to live well as people of virtue and honour.

I have no doubt that Milbank and Pabst's understanding and criticism of liberalism will invite critical responses. 'Things are not that bad,' will be a refrain. After all, liberalism produces people who dismiss strong positions because liberals cannot recognize that they have a strong position. The kind of position Milbank and Pabst represent runs the risk of dying the death of a thousand qualifications, which is the academic equivalent of being nibbled to death by ducks. I have no intention of being part of that flock. That may be because I am in deep sympathy with Milbank and Pabst's understanding and critique of liberalism and with some of their proposed alternatives. By exploring my differences with their recommendations I hope to clarify why I began with a shepherd's story.

Milbank and Pabst call their proposed alternative post-liberalism. Post-liberalism is a blend of two older traditions: 'a combination of honourable, virtuous elites with greater popular participation: a greater sense of cultural duty and hierarchy of value and honour, alongside much more real equality and genuine freedom in economic and political realms' (pp. 1–2). I am particularly drawn to their understanding of the ethics of virtue which they believe reflects nature's goodness found in the purposive ends that are innate in being itself. Those whose lives are so formed when confronted by what may be morally difficult do not ask what should be done, but rather, 'What should I consistently be doing *at all*? What sort of shape might my entire life appropriately take? What sort of character do I want to be and how should I order this desire in an acceptable way to my relationships with others?' (p. 4).

Such questions, and admittedly the authors observe that these are not questions we need to ask on a daily basis, are often raised at crucial transitional points in our lives. I suspect, for example, such a point might be when the newly married couple ask themselves, 'What have we done?', or new parents are suddenly faced with the stark reality that they have brought a new life into the world and are not sure why. Any answer to these questions, moreover, entails further questions about the kind of society in which we want to live. 'How does my life fit with the life of others with whom I must share goods?' is a question that cannot be avoided if we would live lives that can be happily narrated. The good news is that we cannot have an honourable life without others who also seek to live honourably.[14]

To so live can sound quite burdensome, but Milbank and Pabst do not think that is the case. To live virtuously does not mean that we must be constantly thinking about what we should do or not do. Rather, Milbank and Pabst observe that most of what we do that is honourable is 'an everyday matter of performing your job well, being a good lover, spouse, parent, friend, colleague and citizen, or even enjoying a game or a trip. For if goodness is given in nature and not something we contrive with difficulty from time to time, then simple gratitude is a crucial aspect of virtue' (p. 5).

Milbank and Pabst, who know that much of what they are recommending will be viewed as reactionary, do not hesitate to take positions that many will think outrageous. Their defence of an ethics of honour, for example, could be considered as an exercise in nostalgia. Yet they argue, drawing on papal social encyclicals, that a post-liberal ethic is about the everyday process of locating the goods we have in common. Such goods are not, as liberalism would have it, the aggregate of privately owned items, but rather goods that can be shared together, such as intimacy, trust and beauty. The goods that should determine how we live are embedded in the practices of honour and reciprocity that are developed over time through the habits sustained by a tradition. The formation of such traditions depends on the existence of people of wisdom who can provide the judgements necessary for responding to new challenges while remaining faithful to the past (p. 70).

The substitution of technique for wisdom is one of the main reasons why we have no place for understanding the responsibilities and status of the elderly. In wisdom cultures the elderly are expected to remember the judgements made in the past about matters that can be other. Once a social order no longer depends on memory, the old have no responsibility to younger generations. The result, too often, is to make growing old a dreadful development, which may increasingly be understood as an illness. To grow old in societies like the USA means that your primary responsibility is to get out of the way.

Milbank and Pabst's refusal to play at being politically correct is perhaps most clearly on display in their advocacy of Bradley's 'my station and its duties', suggesting the kind of social formations required in order to have the possibility of goods that can be shared. They argue that we need some account of civic roles in order to have a basis for discerning what resources should belong to those who have specific responsibilities. Such judgements inevitably imply the legitimate place for hierarchies and elites for initiating the young into the tradition of the virtues (p. 74). They think that such an ethos and politics is a realistic possibility because increasingly the working class and the middle class share a common commitment to meeting the needs of family and community (p. 76). They argue that a coalition politics so conceived would be an alternative to the liberal commitment to abstract universalism and the corresponding denial of the significance of place.

In support of their views, Milbank and Pabst use George Orwell's socialist vision because of Orwell's emphasis on practices of reciprocity, through gift giving and receiving, which make possible the process of mutual recognition. Orwell rightly thought that most people pursue association with others because they desire that their contribution, no matter how small, to our common life be recognized. To be so acknowledged is what it means to be honoured.

People who so live do not think that their first task in life is to become more wealthy or powerful as individuals. Rather, wealth is best thought of as what we share in common, such as parks, or practices to which all have access, such as medicine. In other words, the post-liberal strategy is exactly the opposite of the liberal assumption that social practices of mutual assistance should be eliminated, while at the same time encouraging our desire for wealth and prestige. The liberal desire for the well-being of the individual not only ignores the goods built on gift relations, it in effect destroys the habits that make such relations possible (p. 79).

To their credit, Milbank and Pabst confront head on what I take to be the most determinative objection to their understanding of post-liberalism: the problem of luck. Luck comes in many forms and sizes but the most fundamental manifestation of luck is the brute fact that no one chooses when, where, or to whom they will be born.[15] Yet the family into which we are born determines our future, making us subject to inequalities that are justified in the name of this or that tradition, history, or some other abstraction.

I have always thought that the profound moral power of the liberal tradition is to be found in the liberal desire to defeat luck. That is particularly the case when luck may be just another name for fate. The impersonality and abstract universalism characteristic of liberal institutions is an attempt to find a way not to let the accidents of birth determine a person's life.[16] Milbank and Pabst, however, argue that liberalism's ambition to overcome luck results in the destruction of any sense that we have a responsibility to fulfil the duties associated with the ascribed roles we inherit through birth (p. 221).

The importance of luck creates the context for Milbank and Pabst's defence of hierarchy and the importance of sustaining an aristocracy governed by a monarch. The defence of hierarchy, they argue, is but a correlative of the necessity for an established Church. If it is not established, the Church threatens to become but another voluntary society, rather than a political entity that is the living heart of the nation (pp. 230–1). Milbank and Pabst develop a complex theological position (complex is my way of saying I'm not sure I 'get it') to argue that the established Church also requires that there be a monarch who can receive the sacraments for the whole society.

Milbank and Pabst defend this account of aristocracy by turning the tables on liberalism. They do so by arguing that the liberal respect for persons *qua* persons can be compatible with the exploitation of the person *qua* miner, *qua* father, and so on. As a result of this false idealism, personhood is divorced from vocational role. But, Milbank and Pabst argue, if Aristotle is right that the aim of politics is to produce virtuous citizens, and since people develop character through social and economic relations, then these relations cannot be attended to properly if virtuous formation of people is not the purpose of politics. This will require that each and every person's contribution to common life be valued in a manner that each person can be assured that they can exercise political influence through their workplace and with those they share a common purpose with (pp. 85–6).

Milbank and Pabst argue that not only is their account of aristocracy consistent with democracy, but in fact democracy is dependent on the existence of elites. Elites are not necessarily incompatible with democracy. What is incompatible with democracy is liberalism, exactly because of the liberal presumption that all forms of hierarchy are arbitrary and unjust. The liberal attempt to destroy aristocratic elites can lead to the tyranny of the majority.

Liberalism and democracy are in tension just to the extent that liberalism results in a populism that is indifferent in matters of truth and goodness. The liberal emphasis on individual preference can result in the spread of a kind of anarchy that 'exacerbates the increasing inability of the modern sovereign state to command the loyalty of its citizens' (pp. 186–7). War becomes the necessary means to secure the obedience of people who have been formed to vote their self-interests.[17]

Storied by Christ

The high theory that Milbank and Pabst represent may seem quite foreign to Rebanks' depiction of the life of a shepherd. I suspect that Rebanks does not need Milbank and Pabst to understand his life. Milbank and Pabst probably do need stories like the one Rebanks tells about his life. They need Rebanks because they need exemplifications of the kind of lives they intimate must exist if their position is to be persuasive. The challenge Milbank and Pabst represent is not that lives such as Rebanks' do not exist, but under the power of the liberal story people like Rebanks may lack the resources to rightly tell the story of their life. Even more troubling, people like Rebanks, and like you and me, may wrongly describe who we have been and who we are yet to be. It is a testimony to his humility and modesty that Rebanks makes neither of those mistakes.

Though I am obviously sympathetic with the general position Milbank and Pabst represent, I think there is something missing in their argument that is not without importance if we are to understand what we need to make our lives our own. What is missing in Milbank and Pabst is a person called Jesus and the people he gathers called the Church. Milbank and Pabst are good Christians, and there is no doubt that Christianity plays an important role in their account of an ethic of virtue and honour. But Christianity is not the Church. The Church is a particular people who have been gathered from the world to worship Jesus. That they do so is the necessary condition for them to have lives that glorify God without their lives being desperate attempts to secure worldly glory.

Milbank and Pabst no doubt assume that such a Church exists, but that Church seems subordinate to a more determinative reality called England. That they have England gives them the confidence that social, economic and political practices are possible at a national level to offer an alternative to liberalism. That is why they contemplate alliances between the working classes and the middle class. I have trouble keeping Blue Labour and Red Tories straight.

All of which means that I am obviously an American. I do not have an England to think about or with. In truth, I am not sure that Milbank and Pabst have the England they seem to think is somehow lurking in the wings ready to be reborn. And this is not irrelevant to the questions about the politics in which we now seem caught. For unless a people exists who have a narrative more determinative than the story shaped by the politics of the day, I fear that we will continue to produce politicians like Donald Trump who are as dangerous as they seem. They are, moreover, all the more dangerous because no people seem to exist capable of telling them the truth. Of course, some quite extraordinary people exist, like the poet and farmer Wendell Berry, but Wendell Berry is not in politics. At least, not in what most Christians in America assume is 'real politics'; that is, the politics of election.[18]

To be a Christian in America is to assume that there is a form of political organization that is not only compatible with our fundamental Christian convictions but is the expression of those convictions. The name for that political reality is democracy. The discipline I represent, Christian ethics, is built on the assumption that American democracy is *the* form of Christian politics. Thus Walter Rauschenbusch, the great representative of the social gospel, would claim that Jesus saved God by taking the Father by the hand and by so doing made God the Father a democratic figure. According to Rauschenbusch, Jesus came proclaiming as well as instituting the kingdom of God to be a movement in history to democratize all our relations with one another. Rauschenbusch could even claim that politics in America had been saved because we were a democracy. The great remaining challenge, Rauschenbusch maintained, was to extend that political transformation to the economic realm.[19]

Though Rauschenbusch's naive underwriting of democracy is often criticized, his fundamental presumption that there is a necessary relation between Christianity and democracy is assumed by subsequent figures identified as theologians and ethicists. Reinhold Niebuhr, one of the sharpest critics of Rauschenbusch, developed a realist justification of democracy that I suspect continues to be assumed by many who seek to express their Christian convictions in a politically significant way.[20] For Niebuhr, democracy was not an ideal, but that is not a problem because there are no ideals. Exactly because there are no ideals is why Christians have a stake in democracy as an expression of the best one can do under the conditions of sin.

What we may now be facing is a challenge to the presumption that democracy is *the* expression of Christian convictions. In 1981 I wrote a chapter in *A Community of Character: Toward a Constructive Christian Social Ethic*, entitled 'The Church and Liberal Democracy: The Moral Limits of a Secular Polity'. In that essay I suggested that the Christian underwriting of democracy as rule by 'the people', when the people are understood to be self-interested players in a zero-sum game of power, has resulted in the loss of voice by

Christians necessary for the Church to be an alternative polity.[21] I continue to think that may be true.

The issues surrounding the relation of Christianity and democracy will not and should not go away. The advent of Trump has raised them with new urgency. In particular, Trump has alerted us again to the worry that there is finally no check on the tyranny of the majority in democracy as we know it. Tocqueville's worry that individualism would undermine American democracy is back on the table. Tocqueville saw clearly that democratic citizens pursuing their own interest without regard for the commonwealth would result in the loss of associational forms of life on which democracy depends. Andrew Sullivan, drawing on Plato's critique of democracy, argued in an article in the *New York Magazine* that democracy depends on elites to protect democracies from 'the will of the people'. Sullivan's position has been countered by Jedediah Purdy, who argues that it is not majoritarian democracy that is the problem but the growing economic power of a small group of capitalists who have the strength to undermine the kind of rule Trump says he is for.[22]

I have no intention of trying to resolve these fundamental questions in democratic theory and practice. I think Milbank and Pabst are right to call attention to the incompatibility of liberalism and some forms of democracy. That does not mean, however, that democracy as identified by John Bowlin as the 'resistance to domination through the practices of mutual accountability' is an ideal whose institutional form it is worth trying to imagine.[23] I fear we are not even close to having such an imagination in play.

But we do have James Rebanks. To have begun a chapter dealing with the challenge of national and global politics by calling attention to Rebanks' account of being a shepherd may seem quite odd. It is odd, but also hopeful. I believe that as long as we can produce narratives of lives like Rebanks', we have a way out of the mess we are in. Alasdair MacIntyre observes that most work is tedious and arduous, but nonetheless fulfilling if the work has a purpose, if it can be recognized as our contribution for doing it and doing it well, and if we are rewarded for doing it in a way that enables the realization of goods of family and community.[24] MacIntyre even suggests that such a conception of work is a form of prayer.

This view of work is why I think it crucial, no matter what you call the systems in which we now find we exist as Christians, that we discover ways to sustain the truthfulness that is constitutive of learning how to be a good judge of sheep. Such a way of life is only made possible by people who have good work to do – work that can only be done if we have the skills to say what is true. Hopefully Christians will be such a people, because God in these times seems to be determined to make us a people who are leaner and meaner. Such a people might know how to tell one another the truth, because we no longer have anything to lose. A people who have nothing to lose, moreover, might discover that we want no other life than the one we have been given.

Notes

1 James Rebanks, *The Shepherd's Life: Modern Dispatches from an Ancient Landscape* (Oxford: Penguin, 2015). Paginations in text.

2 I am not suggesting that Rebanks' declaration is equivalent to him being morally good, though I think he is a person of rare virtue. Interestingly enough, Alasdair MacIntyre comments in his *Dependent Rational Animals: Why Human Beings Need the Virtues* (Chicago: Open Court, 1999) that 'someone can be a good shepherd without being a good human being, but the goods of sheep farming are genuine goods' (pp. 65–6). I am sure MacIntyre is right but I also think the kind of goodness necessary to be a good shepherd puts one on the road to being morally good. I do not think MacIntyre would disagree. Implied in the connection between learning to be a good shepherd and being a good person, however, is the assumption that that may be truer of some tasks than it is of others.

3 Though the phrase is now associated with the white demand to use the police to put African Americans in their place, that was not the original context that gave birth to the phrase. Paul Ramsey pointed out to me that it was first used by African Americans to demand that white police intervene to prevent black on black crime. That was, of course, necessary in a segregated society because in the South police forces that were white simply did not apply the law in African American sections of their towns.

4 One of the questions raised by the Trump phenomenon is what makes the middle class the middle class. There is increasing evidence that the middle class is shrinking.

5 It is interesting to ask what it means for people to want to be 'better off'. Often when asked they say that they would like their children to have more opportunities than they had, but that answer betrays a vagueness about what exactly that would entail. It usually means that they would like for their children not to have to work as hard as they had to work, but it remains unclear what that means in terms of what they would like for their children to get out of life. The oft-made declaration that 'I just want them [meaning their children] to be happy', is not

very informative or helpful. You seldom hear someone say that they want their child to be a good person. I suspect that people do want their children to be good, but that is seldom made explicit.

6 There are several generations – I am part of several – whose moral identity is dependent on having a cause to support. The first cause was the civil rights struggle, then anti-Vietnam, then support of the women's movement, all of which seems to have climaxed with the protest against prejudice towards gays. Each of these movements was worthy of support but they raise very different moral issues. That they do so is often ignored by many people who use the movements to assure themselves that morally they are on the right side of history and thereby morally OK. Their 'personal' life may be a shambles but at least they are politically rightly identified. The continuing tension in American public life between freedom and equality is evident when the reasons for supporting these causes are made articulate. Put differently, when everyone is said to be 'equal' simply as a result of being an American, then the significance of difference – ain't I a woman – is not clear.

7 Alasdair MacIntyre, *After Virtue*, 3rd edition (Notre Dame, IN: University of Notre Dame Press, 2007), p. 34.

8 John Milbank and Adrian Pabst, *The Politics of Virtue: Post-Liberalism and the Human Future* (London: Rowman and Littlefield, 2016). Paginations in text.

9 This is an observation made by Pretty Shield, a Crow Native American, after the destruction of the Crow way of life. Jonathan Lear provides a haunting account of Plenty Coup, the chief of the Crow, in his *Radical Hope: Ethics in the Face of Cultural Devastation* (Cambridge, MA: Harvard University Press, 2006). Lear's account of Pretty Shield is on p. 61.

10 The best account I know of the implications of a global market for how the nation state will be understood is Philip Bobbitt's *The Shield of Achilles: War, Peace, and the Course of History*

(New York: Anchor Books, 2003). The great tension Bobbitt sees clearly is how the developing 'market state' can maintain the honour ethic of the military.

11 Ron Beiner, *What's the Matter with Liberalism?* (Berkeley: University of California Press, 1992), pp. 22–3. For my use of Beiner's account of liberalism see my *Dispatches From the Front: Theological Engagements With the Secular* (Durham, NC: Duke University Press, 1994), pp. 156–63.

12 My usual way of putting this is to say that modernity is the name for the political and economic ambition to produce people who believe that they should have no story other than one they chose when they had none. The only problem with that story is that those to whom it belongs did not choose it.

13 Often those who support the ethos of the Enlightenment argue that figures like MacIntyre continue to presume the goals of the Enlightenment, such as the securing of freedom. They fail, however, to comprehend that what MacIntyre means by freedom is quite different from the view of most Enlightenment thinkers. The latter concentrate primarily on freedom from, but MacIntyre is concerned mainly with freedom for. The same is true of the importance of equality. For MacIntyre the question is how equality works in some social relationships but not in others. Accordingly, from MacIntyre's perspective some account of hierarchy is required. For MacIntyre's reflections on these matters see his 'Where We Were, Where We Are, Where We Need to Be', in Paul Blackledge and Kelvin Knight (eds), *Virtue and Politics: Alasdair MacIntyre's Revolutionary Aristotelianism* (Notre Dame, IN: University of Notre Dame Press, 2011), pp. 326–7.

14 Milbank and Pabst do not provide an extended account of honour, but I take it they are trying to recommend an understanding of honour that simply has no standing in the modern world. At least that is Alasdair MacIntyre's view. In *After Virtue*, MacIntyre argues that the ancient understanding of honour

as the recognition of what is due a person has been lost because any account of our relation to one another as determined by what is due has been abandoned (p. 116).

15 For an extremely important analysis of luck, see Lisa Tessman, *Burdened Virtues: Virtue Ethics for Liberatory Struggles* (Oxford: Oxford University Press, 2005). Tessman develops the notion of moral luck as the presumption that a person of good character has 'responsibilities that outrun control'. Tessman's nuanced account of moral luck turns on how luck shapes as well as is shaped by our lives. She provides an extremely interesting account of the moral damage that comes from being oppressed or being the oppressor. She quite rightly develops Aristotle's insight that good luck can be bad for us if we fail to have the character necessary to receive such a benefit. These are complex but crucial questions that have not been sufficiently explored in contemporary philosophy or theology. For example, we need to know how to think about the significance of the temperament for our being virtuous. Is temperament luck? Tessman distinguishes between constitutive moral luck and luck we associate with being 'lucky'. Temperament seems clearly to be a form of constitutive luck but that makes it no less significant for our becoming persons of moral character. Tessman suggests that regret is crucial for our ability to make our own what may have happened to us, but we must take responsibility for it if we are to have a life worth living.

16 The hegemonic character of liberalism can be made apparent in the language we use that is assumed to be a description of the way things are. For example, the phrase 'accident of birth' is a description shaped by liberal presupposition that there is a non-accidental way to be born.

17 For an account of the place of war as a moral and liturgical enterprise for Americans see my *War and the American Difference: Theological Reflections on Violence and National Identity* (Grand Rapids, MI: Baker Books, 2011).

18 I have often compared American national elections to the Roman use of the staged battle to distract the proletariat from noticing who is ruling them. Elections become a form of entertainment that gives people the mistaken idea that they are ruling themselves because they get to vote. Donald Trump seems to be a confirmation of this understanding of the electoral process. The association of democracies with elections is a profound but widely held mistake.

19 For an account of Rauschenbusch see my chapter 'Walter Rauschenbusch and the Saving of America' in my *A Better Hope: Resources for a Church Confronting Capitalism, Democracy, and Postmodernity* (Grand Rapids, MI: Brazos Press, 2000), pp. 71–108.

20 I have written about Niebuhr's position in a number of essays, but on this matter particularly relevant is my chapter written with Michael Broadway entitled, 'The Irony of Reinhold Niebuhr: The Ideological Character of Christian Realism', in my *Wilderness Wanderings: Probing Twentieth-Century Theology and Philosophy* (Boulder, CO: Westview Press, 1997), pp. 48–61.

21 Stanley Hauerwas, *A Community of Character: Toward a Constructive Christian Social Ethic* (Notre Dame, IN: University of Notre Dame Press, 1981), pp. 72–88.

22 Jedediah Purdy, 'What Trump's Rise Means for Democracy', *Dissent* (4 May 2016).

23 John Bowlin, 'Democracy, Tolerance, Aquinas', *Journal of Religious Ethics*, 44, 2 (May 2016), pp. 278–99.

24 Alasdair MacIntyre, 'Where We Were, Where We Are, Where We Need to Be', p. 323.

4

Beyond fear and discrimination

Sarah Coakley

In this chapter I shall proceed in three moves. First, I want to turn briefly to the biblical source of the question of the 'neighbour' that animates this volume, and perhaps tease a little beyond where Rowan Williams left things. His account of the problem 'Who is my neighbour?' is challenging enough, and focused on the paradox of being able *both* (as he put it) to 'accept the challenge of being a life-giver' *and* to 'accept the gift of a life-giving action towards us by a stranger'.

But I want to locate this biblical conundrum 'Who is my neighbour?' more explicitly in the context of ongoing spiritual practice – in the painful learning of the processes of prayer, moral attention and personal transformation. These are undertakings that may seem merely personal or individualistic at first blush, but as I hope to show, they bleed inexorably into the social and political, the ethical and the legal; and if we continue to harbour some ambition to change the world in the power of the Spirit, then we had better attend to these particular long-haul, ascetic practices of neighbourliness.

But they do not come easily and we need to acknowledge their costliness. We also need to chart how they relate

specifically to the particular topics of 'fear' and 'discrimination'. The first, fear, is a universal aversive experience surely
known to us all, but not always easily understood; the second,
discrimination, is a problem with rather different modern
and ancient semantic associations, but a phenomenon today
by which some of us mete out repression on others, and
often unconsciously.

Such, then, is my first task: to think a little probingly,
or discomfitingly, about what it takes, spiritually speaking,
to follow Jesus' teaching on the neighbour, and how it
involves a process of the difficult undoing of fear and discrimination.

Second, I want to take you on a brief exploration of contemporary evolutionary theory, as it relates to our topic.
This might not seem an obvious point of connection, but I
hope to show that it is. The question that we shall press here
is this: does being a neighbour in Jesus' sense, particularly
as it relates to breaking down fear and discrimination, have
any sort of natural basis in the history of evolution? Or are
humans attempting to swim entirely against the genetic tide
in such a spiritual ambition, as the much vaunted 'selfish
gene' ideology would suggest? In short, is attending to the
neighbour, whoever that is, somehow front-loaded into our
genes, or is it precisely the opposite? And if this attention
to the neighbour does have some sort of 'natural' base, as I
want to argue it does, what can we learn from that and how
far can it take us morally and spiritually?

Third, I attempt to thread the seemingly paradoxical lessons
from our first two sections together, to essay a conclusion

and a final challenge. By this time, we shall have come to find that fear and discrimination have a shared root in the form of a deep human malaise in relation to 'otherness' that is not easily acknowledged, let alone easily healed.

Yet the attempt to fix these problems politically (even universally) by means of an appeal to an 'altruism' founded in rational choice theory, however illuminating such an account may be mathematically, has its own moral difficulties, as we shall see; for it extricates us from the messiness and intimacy of the wounded or needy 'other' in our very midst. It follows in conclusion that the true recognition of the neighbour propels us beyond fear and discrimination only by a sort of ethical excess in the face of the irreducibly specific 'other', in an altruism that Jesus commands us to beyond natural calculation, despite its undeniable *foundation* in the natural, the animal, and the evolutionary.

I will end with a challenge that is simultaneously spiritual, moral and political: how can we be propelled afresh towards such a sacrificial excess of neighbourliness, without which the political and ecological trials of this world in our generation can only intensify and worsen?

Neighbours, fear and discrimination – some biblical and spiritual reflections

Let me start by taking us back to the story of the Good Samaritan in Luke 10.25–37. This is a text that has become perhaps too familiar, and thus no longer as challenging and destabilizing to our modern readership as it should be. I would like to draw attention to just two features of the story in particular, ones that should continue to goad and trouble us as we go forward.

The first is the surprising reversal of the expected identity of the neighbour at the end of the narrative. Initially we think that it is the assaulted stranger who is the neighbour seeking help from the Samaritan; but at the end, Jesus asks, 'Who then was the neighbour to the man who was robbed?' Of course, it is the Samaritan himself. This suggests a strange sort of logic of two-way exchange – each becomes 'neighbour' to the other.

As Rowan Williams put it, it is a matter of 'loving the stranger as one who could save *our* lives'. But I think the story presses us even further than this insight, important as it is. The problem is not just one of recognition of who our neighbour is, but of what I call a sort of necessary 'ecstasy' of response in recognizing her or him (the 'neighbour') beyond family, beyond nation, beyond even favoured religious community. Jesus' ethic of altruistic love is, as we know from many of his other demands (turning the other cheek, loving the enemy), what we might call *excessive* in its demands. Indeed, it might even be thought humanly impossible on any normal rational scale of expectations.

And this is perhaps because it involves breaking down my *own* given, assumed sense of self, in a kind of outgoing movement that was called by Bernard of Clairvaux in the twelfth century an *excessus mentis*[1] – an ecstasy of the mind, towards something unknown, towards the neighbour revealed in *God*, the one who alone can give my identity back to me as *changed.*

So there is a kind of circularity in the ecstasy of going out unexpectedly and newly to the 'other' that we can only make sense of within the context of participation in the divine.

The second feature of the narrative also perhaps insufficiently noted has a correlative aspect. It is when the lawyer correctly answers Jesus that the key to the inheritance of eternal life is to 'love God supremely first and then one's neighbour as oneself'. The lawyer, of course, then goes on to be pedantically bothered about who the neighbour is, but what he does not ask is how he can rightly love *himself* in the first place, for without that he certainly cannot rightly love his neighbour.

It is on this matter too that Bernard of Clairvaux, in that same wonderful text *On Loving God* (*De diligendo Deo*), is so interesting and illuminating, for he insists that the greatest height of love is not simply to ascend to loving God for God's sake, itself a very high state. The higher state still, he says, is rather to come full circle and love *oneself* for God's sake: that is, to find one's true identity in that same contemplative 'excess of the mind' – that ecstasy that flows out of the cramped self of self-loathing and returns to oneself a true account of one's own selfhood *as supremely loved by God*.

It follows that the project of identifying the neighbour is not only a quest for my own selfhood, in that to and fro, but specifically for my own selfhood *as redeemed in God* and knit into relationship with the 'other' in him. I must come to love myself in God *before* I can truly love my neighbour 'as myself'.

Now if this paradoxical rendition of what is happening in that story of the Good Samaritan is right, then how do 'fear' and 'discrimination', specifically, prevent that passage of ecstatic, mutual recognition in God, and how can their taints be expunged?

It is here that the effects of the Fall are so damagingly felt in constraining that capacity for mutual recognition. It is not for nothing that the story of the Fall in Genesis 3 is one of what we might call 'desire gone wrong' in its tragic misdirection (Genesis 3.6). And note that the almost instantaneous effect of this misdirection of desire in the Fall narrative is a blaming of the 'other' – the man of the woman, the woman of the serpent (Genesis 3.12–13).

I have recently discovered a most disturbing late nineteenth-century American interpretation of the Fall, which quite seriously asserted in the wake of Darwin that the serpent was really a black man, half-man, half-beast – the missing link.[2] And who knows but that this hermeneutical manoeuvre of racism does not still tarry somewhere in the white American consciousness.

Fear of the 'other' and blame of the 'other' are thus deeply entangled in the corruption of desire, the essence of all sin according to Genesis 3. And such is felt, I submit, in the body as well as in the mind. I cease to be able to see the 'other' as neighbour in this setting of sin, just as, not unconnectedly, modern pornography trains the falsely objectifying gaze away from intimate recognition of the 'other'.[3] Once our very sensorium is damaged, and brought down into fear, loathing and projection on to the 'other', what can redeem it? 'Perfect love drives out fear', we are taught; but by what *process*?

The early Christian ascetic and monastic writers were deeply engaged with this question, and I believe that their insights remain enduringly significant. Writers such as Evagrius Ponticus in the late fourth century painstakingly systematized the insights of the earlier desert fathers on what he called the 'negative passions',[4] highlighting how such dark thoughts (what the wonderful contemporary spiritual writer Martin Laird OSA calls 'the inner video'[5]) constantly play out in our subliminal consciousness, fuelling fear and prejudice. Yet we cannot dispel such habits by mere acts of will or postures of fortitude. As Evagrius and others teach, it is a matter of a journey in the spirit, into purifying, redeemed stillness – what Evagrius calls 'pure prayer'; this is the only gradual sanctifying process of contemplative attention that can bring about true realism to the 'other'.

But this is a long-term ascetic task. It is not something that can be 'achieved' by mere human goodwill and effort, in the form of the self-produced 'Pelagianism' that Augustine so sternly resisted. As Martin Laird puts it in his book *Into the Silent Land*, learning to practise true attention involves confronting, and diagnosing and resisting, the ever-present temptation to judge others – that is, precisely to engage in 'discrimination' and 'fear'. We will see more clearly only over time, and *through* the patient practices of prayer, what role temptation plays in the circuitry of our struggles, how judgemental thoughts are a mass of anger, fear, envy, pride and shame, which can only be dissipated in what Laird calls 'the ground of awareness'.[6]

Such a ground of awareness arises only through confrontation with our own inner darkness, as the great mystical writers of the later Western Christian tradition, perhaps supremely John of the Cross, also chart in intimate detail. As this journey in prayer continues through its painful, dark nights, the flame of divine love purifies and cauterizes our wounded darkness. What then is felt as the heavy hand of divine judgement, writes John of the Cross, is in reality the lightest caress of divine love.[7] But this is a divine process, a process of contemplation and sanctification infused into us by the Spirit, and undertaken humanly in patience, humility and hope; it is a process in which, as the great twentieth-century African American writer Howard Thurman puts it, 'I let go of my accumulations' of fear and resentment, laying myself lightly into the wind of the Spirit.[8] And as Teresa of Avila remarks in her wonderful 'Seventh Mansions', it is really only in final union with Christ that I can see what it is to love my enemy as my neighbour, as I regain the capacity to pass ecstatically once more out to the 'other's' perspective, and thus find the 'other' written into the logic of divine love.[9]

Now such masters of the spiritual life as these may well seem far beyond our purview or capacity. But my point is that the original desert authors, on which they all build, saw this task of inner transformation in the Spirit as endemic to the Christian life for us all, a *sine qua non* of the ordinary processes of Christian sanctification after baptism.

We need only to lean into that wind of the Spirit and begin to contemplate in truth, and the processes of purgation start. As the St Louis black rapper Tef Poe said at the time of the police shootings there in 2012, racism in America cannot be fixed by political discourses: the modern discourses of 'civil rights' alone will not fix it; manifestly that discourse has failed black people in America. Instead, he says, it is a matter of *seeing* – of having our damaged sensorium withdrawn from the practices of fear, discrimination and resistance, and returned to us in purified form. But that suggestion and possibility has become corrupted and brutalized in us ('black' as well as 'white'), especially in recent years when our sensorium has been overwhelmed by visual overload from the web and the other media, and laced with violence and hatred.[10]

As Rhidian Brook remarked in a fine 'Thought for the Day',[11] even the story of *Cathy Come Home* no longer disturbs us as it did the television public 50 years ago. We have become the slaves of our own wondrous, cultural products – television, advertising, the web and social media, pornography. Only patient practices of silent attention will help us regain our capacity truly to see, to see the 'other' as our neighbour.

With that proposal before us, we move on to my second theme, the evolutionary basis of 'altruism'.

Evolutionary cooperation and its meanings

Such a lesson as I have been charting up to now might *seem* overdemanding and arcane in terms of spiritual practice; but I resist that sceptical interpretation. After all, the regular practice of simple contemplation and its 'naked' attention to God costs absolutely nothing – it's open to everybody and anybody; except, of course, in one sense it can cost *everything.* As T. S. Eliot once put it, it is ultimately the business of choosing to be consumed by either the fire of the Spirit or the fire of divine judgement.[12]

Just as we can train ourselves into blunted sight, so the Spirit consciously invites us, if we allow space for it, to the opposite goal ('beyond fear and resentment'), in recognition of the 'other'. Moreover, as I briefly chart in this section, recent developments in evolutionary theory actually give independent credence to the thought that our inherited animal nature is at least fertile ground for such ecstatic reopening of sight to the 'other', to the neighbour.

Consider for a moment the remarkable case of Wes Autrey.[13] Autrey, an African-American labourer in New York, regularly used the subway to accompany his two young daughters to and from school. They were waiting for a train one day in 2007 when he witnessed a white student, about 20 years old, suddenly having an epileptic seizure. Autrey knew enough medically to help deal with this emergency, while his young daughters stood by in some alarm; but then, as a train approached or was heard coming into the station at speed, the student, recovering a little, staggered to his feet and lurched out on to the track in front of the oncoming train.

Without even a moment's hesitation, and leaving his small daughters to their own devices, Autrey threw himself on top of the student, pressing both their bodies down into the hollow between the tracks. Unable to stop in time, the train passed over the two men, just dirtying Autrey's cap with the grease of its undercarriage. Both men were miraculously unharmed.

Now what are we to make of this little vignette? Perhaps not *too* much;[14] and the story afterwards had some bizarre and rather peculiar later accompaniments, not least because someone called Donald Trump subsequently gave $10,000 to Mr Autrey in celebration of his 'altruism'.

But what catches our imagination here is not so much Donald Trump's prize but Autrey's original, and instinctual, response. There was no time to think. There was no time to protect his daughters. He simply acted in response to another person's danger and distress, in an act that risked his own life. And this story contrasts forcibly, for instance, with an amusing trick played on students in Princeton Theological Seminary in the 1970s. While they were on their way to a preaching class on the Gospel of Luke of all things – they had prepared to preach on the pericope on the Good Samaritan – an actor playing a stricken victim waylaid them on the street. Only the students who were not rushing *urgently* to get to class were inclined to stop to assist.[15]

I think what this tells us is that we may sometimes stop to help when we have time; but if we are preprogrammed into some other activity or deadline, it is very difficult to activate our instinctual responses to neighbourliness. We cannot therefore consistently predict what our evolutionary or instinctive responses may be in such an emergency.

But what we do now know with some predictive accuracy is that our evolutionary history disposes us as much to 'cooperation', so-called (that is, potentially sacrificial acts on behalf of another, even another who is not related to me), as to its opposite (that is, selfishness or 'defection'). Indeed, what we now understand is that the whole of the evolutionary spectrum is a dialectical dance between cooperation and defection, between selfishness and sacrifice.[16]

And this is so despite the strange regnancy of the 'selfish gene' interpretation of Darwin in the late twentieth century, which I think is rapidly being exploded now, and not coincidentally was itself regnant at the time of the great financial boom and bust in the West in the last decades of the twentieth century. 'Selfishness' was economically and evolutionarily adulated; but this came with cost.

The mathematical regularities of evolution in relation to the cooperative function, as explored particularly by my collaborator in America Martin A. Nowak and by the octogenarian E. O. Wilson, can now precisely clarify the conditions in which cooperation can sustain itself and indeed become stable evolutionarily in a population, for the good of all. These recurring mechanisms for the maintenance of cooperation, which evolutionary pundits variously call 'kin selection', 'direct reciprocity', 'indirect reciprocity', 'spatial selection' (where clusters of cooperators stick together) and 'group selection', pertain remarkably right across the evolutionary spectrum, from the level of bacteria right through to humans.

And some species of the higher mammals – meerkats, mole rats and dolphins, for instance, are all extraordinary cooperators – are capable of remarkably sophisticated forms of mutual protection and sacrificial cooperative activity, even when they are not closely related to one another. It follows that there is a natural, evolutionary base for an inherited instinct to recognize and aid the 'other'. Here is a trace, you might say (if you're a theologian), of sacrificial grace still inscribed in our created, evolutionary nature. This surely must be good news.

But there are two problems here which must be noted with full realism, in relation to specifically human cooperation and in connection with the particular problems of fear and discrimination.

First, when the evolutionary inheritance of productive or sacrificial cooperation enters the human realm, it confronts a uniquely human fork of decision. It is not simply hardwired inexorably into a human population, but becomes capable of a dramatic divergence of choice, given the special human capacity for reason, language and intentional freedom. Notice that whereas Autrey simply responded to the instinctual urge to cooperation already written into his nature, most of the Princeton students did not. They wanted to get to class on time. That is, even if we know that cooperation makes sense evolutionarily (that is, populations with too many selfish defectors ultimately destroy themselves, as Darwin seemingly already intuited in his later work[17]), that does not mean that humans will inexorably make a good choice for co-operation, especially if it is actually sacrificial. Indeed, since short-term defection (or short-term selfishness) always benefits those individuals who free-ride on others' goodness, that seemingly 'rational' choice for selfishness for short-term selfish gain is always on offer. And the more I comprehend this possibility, the more I can manipulate it, often justifying it in terms of fear and projection on to a despised 'other' that I need to avoid.

Alternatively, however – and here's a hope – a deeper wisdom and calculation may expose the possibility for human altruism on a grand scale, grander indeed than human cultural evolution has previously ever seen: across races, across religions, and beyond the temporal range of short-term national governments. Indeed, if we do not as humans invest in the possibility for grand-scale cooperation of this sort in the coming decades, our ecological system will be winding down much faster than it otherwise would.

In other words, a new, 'excessive' altruism – a 'super-cooperation'[18] – is potentially on offer given the freedom that we humans have been given. This is not beyond the wit of man or woman in the spectrum of widening evolutionary cooperations in the tree of life. Indeed, only thus, I want to argue, can we confront those greatest threats to our worldwide human flourishing today – the threats of global war, of global terrorism, and of increasing ecological disaster.

Yet the point is this, and it takes us back to the message of the first section: how is our corrupted desire for short-term selfishness to be overcome unless by conditioning patterns and practices of attention and neighbourliness? In other words, we have within us destructive powers far more terrible than any meerkat, mole rat or dolphin *qua* humans, but we also (potentially at least) have the capacity in principle for precisely the opposite, for the 'ecstatic' extension of altruism.

How are we to confront this divergence with the aid of all the new evolutionary understanding we now possess? That is our first problem and challenge.

The second problem is an inverse one. For there is a very seductive danger of a falsely objectified mathematical solution to our current moral malaises, well intentioned to be sure, but weirdly dissociated from the problem of neighbourliness with which we began. Such a danger is brilliantly but peculiarly spelt out in a remarkable and fascinating book by William MacAskill, *Doing Good Better*.[19] MacAskill, on the basis of a narrow utilitarian ethic (fully endorsed by his friend Peter Singer), instructs us in detail how to use our charitable giving in ways that do not entangle us at all with the emotional baggage of affective responses to suffering, but compute quite precisely the short-term good outcomes that our particular amount of charitable money can produce.

There is a lot to be learnt from this book, particularly about how charitable giving is often not very rational – we would not, points out MacAskill, make decisions about our stocks and shares in such emotive terms as those we often used to respond to charity appeals. But what is disturbing about MacAskill's rhetoric is that he does not think that this 'effective altruism' need get tangled up with any cooperative risk or sacrificial loss on our own part at all. Giving, he says, can be happily disassociated from 'sacrifice' (a theme to which he is seemingly averse) if we simply play our cards right, rationally and monetarily; we can 'do good better', as he puts it, without any destabilizing direct encounter with the suffering world we seek to ameliorate, and all simply by investing our money rationally and appropriately.

What is wrong with this? we might ask. This leads to my third and final section. What is wrong with MacAskill's position, it seems to me, is that it falsely averts us from what I call the costliness (the *spiritual* costliness) of ecstatic human cooperation – precisely the costliness that is also encoded in the difficult spiritual process of coming properly to see the feared 'other' as a true neighbour.

Thus, as Sam Wells would put it in the terms of his *Nazareth Manifesto*,[20] this not a virtuous ethic of 'being with' in MacAskill; instead it is a utilitarian ethic of paying for some social change precisely *without* importing my own inner self into the problem that I confront, and thus without confronting my own inner fears and discriminations. Just as human excessive altruism cannot solely be explained in genetic terms (it requires something else out of us in terms of intention and transformation), nor can merely rational choice assessments of charity solve the world's problems without transforming our own personal ethical engagement.

So where does this excursus into evolutionary theory and rational choice utilitarianism leave us? My final section presents some conclusions and challenges.

Returning to neighbourliness – morality and politics beyond fear and discrimination

What I have confronted so far in this chapter leaves us, I think, with a paradox, and a challenge for discussion. On the one hand we have seen that human life is naturally and evolutionarily capable of demanding altruistic sacrifices for the neighbour, and even instinctually produces them under certain circumstances. But for these to become habituated and extensively effective, over time banishing fear and discrimination from our repertoire, we need to talk the language of the first section, that of divine grace, of the 'ecstasy of the mind', in Bernard of Clairvaux's words, that participates in God in finding the neighbour.

This, I have argued, is not an elitist contemplative withdrawal from the political world but a full and demanding sacrificial engagement *with* it. And as the evolutionary theorists of cooperation can illuminate, it is likely to be most effective politically when small, prophetic groups of committed cooperators band together, committed to non-violence, committed to non-discrimination, committed to the banishment of fear, committed to ascetic practice – such that these groups will begin to 'leaven the lump'. This is called 'spatial selection' in the evolutionary spectrum of possibilities – groups of cooperators transforming larger populations.

It is not, therefore, just a matter of wielding once more the language of universal 'human rights', or generic moral responsibilities (in the first legal lesson of tort, the Good Samaritan story is appealed to in defence of good standards of marketing that respect the rights of all consumers[21]). For the 'neighbour' is not merely a generic, universal *anybody*. No, living beyond fear and discrimination is finally impossible without painful, inner, spiritual work, painful renegotiation of the renewed capacity to see the neighbour *right here* as the beloved 'other', beloved in God.

At the end of the fourth century, when Evagrius Ponticus was writing of the evil passions, his contemporary Gregory of Nyssa wrote of learning how to find the face, the *prosopon*, of Christ in the leprous faces of beggars in the streets

of Constantinople.[22] Here, he said, was the suffering neighbour offering Christ back to the attentive neighbour, in an
endless circle of Christic negotiation. I am ecstatically
enabled to love my neighbour as myself because I am now
given back my true, Christic self by the neighbour-in-God;
and from here I learn how to banish fear and for the first
time truly to love myself as seen by Christ.

It follows that living beyond fear and discrimination,
although we may legislate for it as well as we can within our
legal and political systems (and, of course, need to continue
to do so, with great commitment), is finally a grace, not a
skill – an enterprise of redeemed Christian sonship, groaned
into by the Spirit in acts of repeated prayer, contemplation
and attention.

But is this *really* possible? This is the challenge laid before
us. For the question summons and challenges all our
resources of Christian faith, hope and love.

Notes

1 See Bernard of Clairvaux, *On Loving God* (available online
  in *Christian Classics Ethereal Library*, <www.ccel.org>),
  section X.
2 For a discussion of the trajectory of this late nineteenth-century
  interpretation of Genesis 3, see David N. Livingstone, *Adam's
  Ancestors: Race, Religion and the Politics of Human Origins*
  (Baltimore, MD: Johns Hopkins University Press, 2008), ch. 7,
  especially pp. 191–200.
3 For an electrifying philosophical analysis of the corruption of
  the human gaze towards an insensitivized 'objectification'
  of the body of the 'other' in pornography, see Rae Langton,

Sexual Solipsism: Philosophical Essays on Pornography and Objectification (Oxford: Oxford University Press, 2009).

4 For the best first taste of Evagrius' spiritual writing on passions, (negative) 'thoughts' and asceticism, see *The Philokalia: The Complete Text*, vol. 1, tr. and ed. G. E. H. Palmer, Philip Sherrard and Kallistos Ware (London: Faber, 1979), pp. 29–71.

5 See Martin Laird OSA, *Into the Silent Land: A Guide to the Christian Practice of Contemplation* (New York: Oxford University Press, 2006).

6 Laird, *Into the Silent Land*, especially ch. 7 and p. 126: 'One of the most precious things we learn is noncondemnation. When we see the judgmental thoughts finally disappear in the ground of awareness, much of what had seemed worthy of condemnation now seems just right the way it is . . . Thorns are as much a part of a rose as the flower.'

7 This, according to John of the Cross, is an essential (albeit experientially paradoxical) part of the second 'night' of the 'spirit', in which – after the senses have been purified by dark contemplation in the 'night of sense' – God probes more deeply into the human spirit to expose and purify its moral turpitude, as if it were a log thrown into the fire: see *The Collected Works of St. John of the Cross*, tr. Kieran Kavanaugh OCD and Otilio Rodriguez OCD (Washington, DC: ICS Publications, 1991), *Dark Night*, book II, pp. 154–265.

8 See Howard Thurman, *Deep is the Hunger: Meditations for Apostles of Sensitiveness* (Richmond, IN: Friends United Press, 1978), 'I let go of my accumulations', pp. 201–2.

9 See *The Collected Works of Teresa of Avila*, tr. Kieran Kavanaugh OCD and Otilio Rodriguez OCD, vol. 2 (Washington, DC: ICS Publications, 1980), *The Interior Castle*, VII, pp. 427–50.

10 For an introduction to Tef Poe's thinking and influence, see <https://en.wikipedia.org/wiki/Tef_Poe>.

11 I believe this was on the morning of 20 October 2016, on *Today*, Radio Four, just before 8 a.m.

12 T. S. Eliot, 'Little Gidding', IV.

13 There is plenty of material on the web about Autrey, starting with: <https://en.wikipedia.org/wiki/Wesley_Autrey>.

14 It will be clear from the web coverage that this unusual incident has received an unexpected amount of attention, some of it projective. One item of information that is relevant is that Autrey did already know in principle (having worked on the metro previously) that it was *just* possible for a person to lie down on the track safely under an incoming train. He could not have known, however, that *two* people could so survive in these conditions.

15 Some details of this interestingly contrived experiment can be found at <http://faculty.babson.edu/krollag/org_site/soc_psych/darley_samarit.html>.

16 What follows draws on my Gifford Lectures of 2012, *Sacrifice Regained: Evolution, Cooperation and God*, at <www.abdn.ac.uk/gifford/about/> (forthcoming Oxford: Oxford University Press/Grand Rapids, MI: Eerdmans, 2018).

17 See John Hedley Brooke, '"Ready to Aid One Another": Darwin, Nature and Cooperation', in Martin A. Nowak and Sarah Coakley (eds), *Evolution, Games, and God: The Principle of Evolution* (Cambridge, MA: Harvard University Press, 2013), pp. 37–59, for a discussion of Darwin's late intuitions on the question of the evolutionary significance of 'sacrifice'.

18 This is Martin A. Nowak's appellation: see his *SuperCooperators*, with Roger Highfield (New York: Simon and Schuster, 2013).

19 William MacAskill, *Doing Good Better: A Radical New Way to Make a Difference* (London: Guardian Books, 2015).

20 See Samuel Wells, *A Nazareth Manifesto: Being with God* (Oxford: Wiley, 2015), especially ch. 1, pp. 11–19.

21 See the famous 1932 Donoghue vs Stevenson 'snail in the bottle' case, in which the Good Samaritan text was appealed to by Lord Atkins as an exemplar for his controversial 'neighbour principle': <http://lawgovpol.com/case-study-donoghue-v-stevenson-1932/>.

22 I discuss Gregory of Nyssa's remarkable understanding of this point in my essay, 'The Identity of the Risen Jesus: Finding Jesus Christ in the Poor', in Beverly Roberts Gaventa and Richard B. Hays (eds), *Seeking the Identity of Jesus: A Pilgrimage* (Grand Rapids, MI: Eerdmans, 2008), pp. 301–19.

5

The cost of reconciliation

Justin Welby

Shortly before I was installed as the Archbishop of Canterbury, one of my colleagues at Lambeth Palace organized a prayer pilgrimage with a number of cathedrals in the southern part of England. The structure of the pilgrimage was very simple. It was announced that I would be in a given cathedral on a given day, between 10 a.m. and 4 p.m., and that anyone was welcome to come and pray with me. We decided in advance that if no one came it didn't matter; at least God would show up.

In our preparation and planning for the pilgrimage, we joined with a group called 24/7 Prayer, a global movement of prayer started by Pete Greig. This extraordinary movement is youth-based and prayer-centred, and engages principally with the most unchurched people around. It is well used to organizing weeks of prayer, and it estimated, with great celebration, that as many as 800 or 900 people would come to the different prayer days in total during the prayer pilgrimage week. The reality, to their surprise – and my astonishment – was nearer 12,000.

The last day of the pilgrimage was at Chichester. The cathedral was heaving with people, and I was wandering around dressed, as usual, in a black cassock and pectoral cross. A man came up to me as I wandered, and said, 'I understand the Archbishop of Canterbury is here today.' I tried to look as modest as possible, although secretly I was rather pleased, and replied, 'Oh, yes, he is.' He answered, 'Is there any chance you could introduce me to him?' At this point I drew myself up to my full 5 feet 8 and a half inches – when you're my height, the half matters – and said, with a decent level of modesty, I hope: 'Actually, it's me.' He looked me up and down, and said, 'Oh.' And he wandered away without another word.

I've been dining out on that anecdote for a while now, and it is precisely true. The point is this: underlying that moment was a question of identity. Who was he expecting to meet? And who did I think I was?

The foundation of our identity

The danger of forming our identity on the temporal and the provisional is enormous. It can overwhelm us. Someone asked me recently, 'What does it feel like to be Archbishop of Canterbury?' The honest answer is, I never 'feel' like the Archbishop of Canterbury. In fact even to ask the question is fairly meaningless, as I have no idea what an Archbishop of Canterbury feels like. Whatever may be the case, we project our understandings of other people's identities on to them, without knowing what it is like to be inside their skin. We can't get past someone else's face. We can see them, we can face them, we can love them, we can know them. But we can never feel what they are feeling. We can only empathize through our own framework of understanding of life and our own identity. And whatever else that is, it is not their identity.

That is the complexity of identity. But in prayer we grow into a place where the identity that is ours in Christ becomes the root and foundational identity on which everything else is built. In Revelation 2.17 the glorified Christ in his letter to the church of Pergamum says this: 'I will give a white stone, and on the white stone is written a new name that no one knows except the one who receives it.' In other words, Christ will give the people their identity; and it is clear that he will do so lavishly and excessively. Read the words of the theologian and poet Ephrem the Syrian from the fourth century:

> The Lord of all
> is the treasure store of all things,
> upon each according to his capacity
> He bestows a glimpse
> of the beauty of His hiddenness
> of the splendour of His majesty.
> He is the radiance who, in His love
> makes everyone shine –
> the small with flashes of light from Him,
> the perfect with rays more intense,
> but only His child is sufficient
> for the might of His glory.[1]

The whole process of developing our individual and corporate identity is one that has to be rooted in prayer, in partnership with this luxurious creator of who we are: with Jesus himself.

And identity is something that is both real and latent potential in all of us. It is real because we are who we are and we exist, and we relate. (We always need to go back to the South

African expression of *ubuntu*: I am because I am in relationship with others.) But it is potential because the foundational, cornerstone identity that we have is the one we have in Christ, and it is always being formed. That is true for every human being, whatever they are like. There are no exceptions. It is not a matter of capacity or incapacity, of colour or ethnicity, of intelligence or ability, of aptitude or disability, of sexuality or character. Our identity is a treasure that is in the purpose of God and exists potentially and actually. Our lives are the forming of that identity.

But what has all this to do with reconciliation? Reconciliation with God through Christ is the process by which we find and grow into our true identities, and through reconciliation we are called to be stewards of the identity of other people.

The treasure of identity

Recently, Caroline and I were in Goma in the Democratic Republic of the Congo, on the far eastern side of the country. There we met an old friend, a local Anglican clergyman, and from there I went with him to an internally displaced persons (IDP) camp. That part of eastern Congo has been in some kind of conflict for over 40 years, and the DRC's casualties, directly and indirectly from that war, are estimated to be between four and five million. To put that in perspective, that is four times the number of British dead in the Great War.

The IDP camp was set on volcanic rock with tents perched on it. It was very hot and very dry, and the ground was awful. Food supplies were not coming in, and there was growing alarm about the shortage of food. Twenty-five thousand people were living in closely packed tents with inadequate sanitation.

At one corner of the camp was a large marquee. In it a doctor was looking after children with varying levels of disability who had become lost or been abandoned by their parents. They lay on the ground or on very thin mattresses. I walked around and came across two small children: a boy perhaps two or three years old and his baby sister. The tiny baby was lying listlessly on her back. She was unresponsive and had significant disabilities. Her sibling sat near her, watching her. I knelt down next to them, and held the little one's hand while I prayed for them. Elsewhere in the camp there was an elderly lady who was blind. She was by herself in her tent and I went in. She was weeping helplessly because she didn't know where she was, her family was nowhere around and she was at the end of her life. I talked to her for a while – but of course she understood nothing; perhaps a touch.

What war does is to take people's identities and tear them apart. Twist them, break them. It is the opposite of the stewardship of the identity of the other; it is its destruction, its disintegration. It does the exact opposite of what God does for us in Christ. And the same, tragically, is true to a greater or lesser extent within households, or communities. It's true when children or vulnerable adults are abused.

In the Church, worst of all when there is disruption and dispute, we cease to treasure the identity that Christ has given to each other, and determine to impose our own understanding of Christian identity on them, or to expel them. One only has to say it to see what a blasphemy this is, what an atrocious kind of behaviour; and yet it seems deeply imbued by the Christian spirit. It is our sin and our wickedness that leads us all at some point in our lives to varying degrees of this sort of behaviour. It is known as demonizing the other, diminishing their identity to the point where it is seen only as darkness, as the absence of God. It's why I'm so passionate about not expelling people. Of course we differ and disagree, and of course that leads to argument, to disruption. But when David Porter, the Director of Reconciliation and later the chief of staff at Lambeth, who has a long history in Northern Ireland, and I speak of 'good disagreement' or 'disagreeing well', it's not a cheap way of saying, 'Let's pretend we don't have problems.' It's a way of saying, 'Identity is precious – not to be twisted and fractured and tortured – because it is God-given.'

Reconciling ourselves with God

Reconciliation comes in two axes. The vertical axis is the relationship with God, which forms and creates and settles our true identity that only he knows, and begins the process of us being enabled to discover that identity. The horizontal axis comes from life lived in this world in community, in prayer together, but is much more than that; it extends into every part of our lives and activities, churchy and non-churchy. Reconciliation is the process by which we learn to treasure the identity of the other.

To treasure someone else's identity does not mean accepting all they do, or agreeing with them unconditionally. That would be absurd. Reconciliation is never about unanimity.

The vertical axis sets the model for the horizontal axis. In the vertical axis God sees all our faults and failings, our sins and our wickedness, and yet loving us gives his Son so that we might know him. The love of Christ, as Paul says in 2 Corinthians 5.14, in the old translation, 'constrains us' (in the NRSV, 'urges us on') into a relationship with God. The love of Christ shapes and makes us. In that reconciliation with God we are rescued from slavery to all the other identities that somehow seek to dominate us, including especially the ones we don't like, the identity that leads me into behaviour that I despise and turn from, and yet turn back to so often.

But such is the nature of the vertical reconciliation. It takes us with all we are and fail to be. Samuel Wells, in a lecture at Coventry Cathedral, started by saying: 'Reconciliation is the Gospel.'[2]

So reconciliation with God, the vertical axis, is something that is absolutely fundamental and essential to our living as Christians, and to being reconcilers. We first have to be reconciled with God. Paul describes this vividly a few verses later: 'So if anyone is in Christ, there is a new creation: everything old has passed away; see, everything has become new!' (2 Corinthians 5.17).

The importance of this reconciliation is impossible to exaggerate. It is essential because it enables us to be who we are called to be, fully alive human beings. That completeness of life is true not only for the individual but also for God's people taken together. We are only truly a community as the Church when we are a community alive in Christ. And we are only truly a community alive in Christ when we are reconciled to Christ and thus to each other, and are reflecting the reconciling character of God in being reconcilers, each of us. Reconciled reconcilers.

In this vertical axis we see the true cost of reconciliation; for it to bring life it costs even the life of the Son of God, and when we speak of reconciliation it must never be cheap, a sort of subfusc getting on with each other. Reconciliation with others costs us what it cost God to be reconciled with us: which is everything.

But the vertical axis of reconciliation is not so much an axis as a fire hose. God pours reconciliation into us in enormous flooding volumes, and into his Church with such force and such overwhelming generosity that it is impossible for us to contain it within ourselves. Therefore the nature of God's people, the Church, should be, as a key sign of them being truly alive in Christ, that they are reconcilers in the world around. We should spray peace and reconciliation everywhere we live.

Reconciling ourselves with others

The horizontal axis of reconciliation is the one in which we begin the process of caring for, stewarding and guarding the identity of others. It is extraordinary when you see it at work. The tent near Goma that I mentioned earlier was operated by a Christian charity supported by Tearfund, called Hope Africa. The money originated with the UK government Department for International Development, and comes out of the 0.7 per cent of GDP that goes on international development. Amid the trauma of that war, this charity has sought to value and guard the identities – to the extent they could considering the overwhelming numbers – of those in the tent and in the camp.

Reconciliation overflows and operates at the most local and the most global levels. At the very local, the Dover Foodbank recently demonstrated a reconciliation in which people were reconciled to their intrinsic value. One man came into the foodbank with his eyes down, so ashamed was he to need to be there, but went out saying: 'This is not a box of food; it's a box of love.'

In many schools, such as the Church of England secondary school in south London I visited several months ago, we see the leadership bringing people together from incredible diversity into a commonality of view, based around clear Christian values and worship, even though many of the children are from other faith backgrounds. Christianity is not imposed, but the structure of Christian faith enables those there to find their identities treasured and the opportunity to grow permitted.

While there, I led an assembly on reconciliation, and then spent 45 minutes with a group of around 15 students of all secondary school ages, while they posed questions and made comments. They were unbelievably articulate, thoughtful and considerate of each other's views, despite the most foundational differences. They were transparently honest about the differences, yet they managed to indicate a respect for each other and a value for each other. I came away deeply encouraged, having seen Christ at work through the leadership and the example and the structure put in place by the teachers there. Identities treasured.

Developing reconciliation

But how do we let reconciliation overflow? I have split this section into six words, all beginning with 'R', that speak of a pattern of developing reconciliation. And we see these Rs above all in the life of Jesus.

Researching

The first word is researching, getting to know. The nature of God is to know us and to know who we are, to understand everything about us to our deepest level, including the things we have no idea about ourselves. Yet with all that, it is not enough. He takes human form and lives with us knowing every temptation, tempted in every way, as it says in the letter to the Hebrews, 'as we are, and yet without sin' (4.15). What is the purpose of the incarnation, or *a* purpose of the incarnation? It is to be like us, so that we can find our identity in him and become like him. The identification with humanity is completed in facing betrayal and loss, torture and death.

Reconciliation on the horizontal axis begins with the process of researching, of sitting alongside, of being incarnational, of experiencing what the other experiences – or, if you are the person seeking to bring reconciliation, what both sides are experiencing, of living in the reality of their dispute; yet 'without sin'. It is not to seek to be objective, not merely to empathize, but to feel at the deepest level. It is to know within oneself the agony of their separation and hatred or dislike or disruption, which is damaging their identities. It is costly.

The first part of any reconciliation action is to know that we don't know. I first went to Nigeria in December 1978, when I was in the oil industry, and from then for the next couple of years I went more or less once a month. At that time I felt I pretty well understood the country. And since 2002 I've also gone quite regularly, yet I know now that even after this great number of years I don't understand anything about the country. The move from unconscious ignorance to conscious ignorance is the first step for the human being in reconciliation. For Jesus that did not exist, thankfully, but for us it does. In the incarnation we see his knowledge lived out in experience, and that calls us to seek knowledge through living in experience with those caught up in conflict, whether in a family or a community, a church or a country.

Relationship

The second R is relationship. John 13.1 tells us that Jesus, knowing who he was and where he had come from, and having loved his disciples, 'loved them to the end'. There are lots of key words in that verse, but love is a pretty good one. That love to the end, to the end of his life, to the limits of love, the end of love, sets the standard of relationships in reconciliation.

Canon Andrew White, the 'Vicar of Baghdad', is an extraordinary man with whom I worked for two years when I was at Coventry. I think the most extraordinary part about him

113

is his capacity to love. That capacity to love, the genuineness of that love for those with whom he deals, means that he is able to build relationships with people at a very deep level, very quickly. Bitter enemies find that both sides are loved by him, and thus a bridge begins to build, built of love, a living bridge which is the reconciler (although remember that the nature of bridges is that they get walked all over; that is the cost of reconciliation). The building of genuine relationships that exist for themselves and not in some manipulative way for the greater good (that dangerous phrase) is core to reconciliation. It is the way God works with us. Romans 5.8 reads: 'But God proves his love for us in that while we still were sinners Christ died for us.' It is the nature of building our identities that we exist in relationship with Christ while yet being sinners. His love overcomes the sin. In the relationship with enemies there will thus always be pain and cost, of our sin and failings as reconcilers and cost for the parties themselves.

Relief

At the Last Supper, we see Jesus recognizing the needs of his disciples and meeting those needs. He washes their feet to meet the need for their pride to be set aside. He gives a memorial to meet their need to know that he is always with them. He teaches them, to meet their need to understand what is about to happen. In every conflict there is need at a deep level of identity; there's a part of the identity that has a gap, a hole, a crack, a need for healing, which requires filling for reconciliation to happen. Even the wealthiest and most successful have some kind of need. Reconciliation involves the essential aspect of meeting need, but to know it we have to have built relationships and done our research. Relieving need is the clearest evidence of true love. Relief does not buy relationship: it demonstrates it.

Risk

In order to let reconciliation flow, we must take risks. Jesus took the greatest risk of all, surrendering himself to those who would torture and then kill him, trusting that God would raise him up and that our salvation would be achieved.

All reconciliation involves taking profound risk. There is an obvious risk to being in areas of conflict, but the greater risk is the risk for us and for the parties in dispute in bringing together people who hate one another. Even to be involved in domestic disputes or community quarrels involves risk: the risk of being the bridge that is hated by those who do not wish to cross it. It takes a long time to get to the point where they will meet. Yet, with those risks is the opportunity for the respect and treasuring of identity.

In 2004 I was on one of a number of visits to Burundi towards the end of the civil war, for a meeting of rebel and government leaders, both civil and military, which I was facilitating. It was three days of working on reconciliation, after a war that had killed 7 per cent of the population. It was hard and grinding conversations, all conducted in French. On the last day a senior officer of one side stood, pointed across the room at another man, and said: 'That man killed 30,000 people through his militia. How can we ever be reconciled?' That comment set out the cost of reconciliation for those in conflict. It is the forgiveness of sin, the decision to move forward and see the price as paid. Reconciliation is so costly that it is very, very rare. You may have peace, but not often reconciliation. I return to this point below.

Reconciliation

The fifth R is reconciliation itself. It's a fragile plant in the cold climate of human identity. It has to be nurtured and protected, guarded and respected, and it's a slow grower. As someone once said to us, about a different subject: 'Weeds spring up overnight; oak trees take centuries.' Reconciliation is an oak, but not as strong. A good rule of thumb is that a week of conflict gives you a year of work on reconciliation. Try applying that to the Middle East, or to Northern Ireland. Each act of nurturing reconciliation costs us our own pride – our own pride in our own identity – as we are shaped into being reconciled reconcilers. Each step forward involves a surrender of self.

The greatest reconciliation in European history came in the second half of the twentieth century. During that period people who had killed millions of each other's citizens learnt to live together and put aside weapons and any thought of war. I remember a French friend of mine, a senior manager at ELF, whose grandfather had been in the Franco-Prussian war, his uncle had been killed in the Great War, his brother in the resistance in the Second World War, in which he'd also fought as a teenager, saying to me: 'You British don't understand Europe. It's nothing to do with economics; it's about not killing.' And that pointed me to that extraordinary moment of reconciliation, so that nowadays the battle is really only carried out on the football field.

But reconciliation remains a fragile flower, and generations that grow up not remembering the hatreds of the first half of the twentieth century, which sprang from 1,500 years of almost continuous war in northern and north-western Europe, may well find that the plant is more fragile than it looks. Look at what happens when we don't nurture reconciliation and see that it's a process not an event. Look at what happens in families when there are damaging quarrels that are not properly addressed. The scars remain, and reconciliation grows around and over them: but they are always there. The process lasts a lifetime, whether it's with God or with each other. There is cost to this day in Europe.

Resourcing

Last, reconciliation needs resourcing. It is something that we have to work at day by day, but to do this we need to find resources. Jesus in John's Gospel promises his disciples the Holy Spirit who will lead them into all truth and equip them to find the identities they are called to have. They will not be left comfortless but will be resourced. With each other we need to encourage and resource, never imagine that once some kind of agreement is made that is the end. We must tend and nurture reconcilers, and strengthen the reconciled. The cost is endless commitment.

Reconciliation is an extraordinarily complex process because it is a process of nurturing identity into health and away from damage, but at its heart is the simplicity of being good stewards of the identity of the others. That definition applies in every area, including the environment where we are called to be good stewards, to be reconciled to the natural world.

It applies especially in the agony of human conflict, from the home to the global fields of battle, in which our deep-set tendency to destroy and twist other human beings' identities is to be replaced by the overflowing waters of the love of Christ, in which by being reconciled reconcilers we imitate our own reconciliation with God and in which we will pay any cost to achieve the goal: that goal of human beings in their own identity – free, reconciled and living to the glory of God.

Notes

1 Ephrem the Syrian (fourth-century theologian in what is now Turkey), *Hymns on Paradise*, trans. by Sebastian Brooke (New York: St Vladimir Press, 1997). Reproduced by permission.
2 Faith in Conflict Conference, Coventry, Tuesday 26 February 2013, 'The Exasperating Patience of God'.

6

Welcoming angels unawares
Abraham, the stranger and the refugee crisis

Megan Warner

Do not neglect to show hospitality to strangers, for
by doing that some have entertained angels without
knowing it.   (Hebrews 13.2)

It should not perhaps be entirely surprising that the letter
to the Hebrews is the most 'Hebrew' of the epistles. The
first 12 chapters of Hebrews look back constantly to Israel's
history in order better to explain and situate the present.
Suddenly, at the beginning of the final chapter, there is a
change. The word 'therefore' alerts the reader that what has
gone before is background and that what follows is, in some
sense, the point. What follows is a piece of wisdom literature
(not unlike the book of Proverbs) in which the reader is
offered a series of exhortations, most with explanations of
the value of adopting a particular action or attitude. The
opening exhortation is simply, 'Let mutual love continue.'
The verse quoted above, Hebrews 13.2, concerning offering
hospitality to strangers, is followed by further practical steps
towards the promotion of mutual love, such as remembering prisoners, honouring marriage and avoiding excessive
love of money. The fact that the letter to the Hebrews is
steeped in Israelite history, religion and literature in this way
makes it possible to assert with some degree of confidence
that Hebrews 13.2 alludes to two stories of hospitality from

chapters 18 and 19 of Genesis. These two stories tell of
occasions when Abraham and his nephew Lot offered hospitality to strangers, with dramatic results. Together these
two stories have a great deal to tell us about hospitality and
the very real chance that, in offering hospitality to strangers,
we may find ourselves entertaining angels unawares.

By the oaks of Mamre

The opening of Genesis 18 finds Abraham sitting at the
entrance of his tent in the heat of the day. The narrator tells
the reader that the LORD appeared to Abraham there, but
almost immediately mystery surrounds Abraham's visitor.
When Abraham looks up he sees not a single divine figure,
but rather three men standing before him. His immediate
reaction is to jump up and rush out to greet the men, bowing deep to the ground in a gesture of respect, and urging
them to turn aside from their journey to join him for a meal.
Abraham's quick and generous response can deflect attention
from the mystery at the heart of the story. The ambiguity
surrounding the identity of Abraham's visitors (or visitor?)
continues throughout, highlighted by the fact that Hebrew
pronouns distinguish between singular and plural in ways
that English pronouns do not. Sometimes, for example, the
story refers to a single visitor ('My lord, if I find favour
with you [singular], do not pass by your servant') and sometimes to three ('So they said, "Do as you have said"'). These
alternative realities – one divine visitor or three human – are
in tension throughout the story, but there is an almost imper-
ceptible shift so that a stronger impression of three human
visitors at the beginning of the story gives way to an impression of one divine guest by its end.

Christian readers have tended to resolve the mystery by identifying Abraham's visitor(s) as the Holy Trinity. This is a
neat solution – one LORD, three persons. Andrei Rublev's
famous Trinity icon depicts the three persons of the Trinity
sitting in a circle around a table at a kind of divine 'tea party',
in which one seat is left vacant for the 'reader' of the icon
to join in. Rublev, no less than the author of the letter to
the Hebrews, was influenced by the Genesis 18 story of
Abraham's hospitality, and in some versions of the icon Sarah
and Abraham are depicted serving their guests at table.

In some respects it does not assist us to identify Abraham's
visitor(s) too readily with the Trinity. It certainly wasn't the
conscious intention of the author of Genesis 18 (writing
centuries before Christ) to write about the Holy Trinity, no
matter how divinely inspired the story, and when the mystery
is left open there is space to appreciate elements of the story
that might otherwise be obscured. For example, although the
reader knows the true identity of Abraham's visitor(s),
Abraham sees only strangers. In that light, Abraham's response
appears extraordinary. He greets the strangers with the
greatest honour and offers them lavish hospitality including
a meal that in his context could best be described as extrava-
gant. He arranges for cakes, curds, milk and a calf to be served
to these three men whom he has never before met.

Abraham's generous response is best appreciated when it
is remembered that Genesis tells this story in relation to
Abraham only once, so it is easy for the reader to assume
that these circumstances happened only once. The reality is
that for somebody in Abraham's position this is a scenario
likely to have played itself out time and time again. The

arrival of travelling strangers in the vicinity of Abraham's tent would have been a relatively common occurrence. Could Abraham really have responded in this conspicuously generous manner each time strangers passed by? It is hard to think so, yet the logic of the story is that Abraham had no reason to know that these visitors were different from any others.

Some historical background may be of assistance here. Research suggests that the situation depicted in the story is typical for the time and area in which Abraham is said to have lived, and that in offering hospitality to these three strangers Abraham was playing his part according to a well-established and well-understood hospitality code. In Abraham's time and context travel was very different from travel today. It generally happened on foot and journeys could take many days. There were no supermarkets or hotel chains, so travellers had to rely on hospitality offered by those living in the areas through which they travelled, or resort to theft and violence. There was a carefully constructed code that governed the way in which such hospitality was offered and accepted – everybody knew it and everybody played their part. The rules were well established; a host need not offer hospitality and a guest need not accept it, but once hospitality had been offered and accepted it had to run a certain course. The host should offer the most generous hospitality they could properly afford. The guest, having accepted, was required to accept whatever standard of hospitality was offered. A guest should not ask for anything additional and should be careful even to refrain from admiring any object in the host's tent, lest the host feel obliged to make a present of it! The guest should not overstay their welcome and at the end of the stay should offer the host a gift. This was typically small and might amount merely to a story or a piece of news from home.

The point of the gift, and indeed of the entire code, was to balance the transaction between host and guest. It was vital that both parties felt they had gained something from the transaction and that neither felt exploited, so that host and guest parted on equal terms. Why was this important and what did the host have to gain from offering hospitality to strangers in such circumstances? In a setting in which significant numbers of people (usually men) were travelling long distances by foot it was as important to the residents of the areas through which they travelled as to the travellers themselves that the travellers got some sleep and had plenty to eat. Tired and hungry strangers represented potential dangers to tent-dwellers. Offering hospitality was a way of converting potential threats into benign passers-by and potential enemies into friends.

Abraham, then, plays his role according to the hospitality code of his day, but he plays it lavishly. Abraham's guests also play their role lavishly. At the end of the meal, before their departure, they present a gift – a promise that Abraham will have a son by Sarah. Abraham's lack of a son and heir has been the tension driving the entire story to this point. The very first thing we learn about Abram (Abraham's name prior to Genesis 17) is that his wife Sarai is barren (Genesis 11.30). In Genesis 16 Abram and Sarai take the initiative (in light of the LORD's apparent inactivity) in arranging for Abram to get a son by Sarai's Egyptian maid Hagar as surrogate. The plan is successful but does not go smoothly.

Now the visitors are promising Abraham and Sarah a son of their own. The gift is not easily accepted, however. Sarah, hearing the promise from the entrance to the tent, becomes frightened and in her fear she laughs (Genesis 18.12). She cannot believe what she is hearing – at her 90-plus years and after all this time barren, is she really to have a child? (In the Hebrew she asks, 'Am I to have pleasure?') When the visitor (there seems to be just one now) asks after Sarah and her laughter, Sarah panics and denies that she laughed (Genesis 18.15). The visitor knows better: 'Oh yes, you did laugh' (Genesis 18.16).

Although it is never said explicitly, it is implied that Sarah and Abraham come to know the identity of the stranger(s) by the end of the story. Both understand eventually that these are no ordinary strangers who have stopped by the entrance to their tent in the heat of the day, but that it is the LORD (probably, as we shall see, accompanied by two angels). At what point in the story does the penny drop? That is the $64,000 question, but there is no definitive answer in the story, or any strong consensus among biblical scholars. Probably the realization is gradual so that there is no one moment when realization comes. The only thing that can be said with any degree of certainty is that at the beginning of the story Abraham and Sarah do not know the identity of their visitor(s), but by the end of the story they do, and this gradual realization is mirrored in the text, as plural pronouns imperceptibly give way to singular. In sum, Abraham receives the strangers as if they are kings, or gods, only to discover that they really are God and that the gift these particular visitors bring far outshines even the extraordinary lavishness of his hospitality.

This is the point picked up by the writer of the letter to the Hebrews – that by extending hospitality to strangers one might find oneself entertaining angels unawares. He and Rublev were not the only ones to be influenced by the story of Abraham's hospitality in Genesis 18, however. The story also undoubtedly influenced St Benedict in constructing his sixth-century 'rule' for monastic life, foundational not only for his own order but for monasticism more generally. Chapter 53 exhorts followers of the rule to offer hospitality to strangers and to recognize Christ in the stranger who comes seeking shelter and food:

> All guests who present themselves are to be welcomed as Christ, for he himself will say: I was a stranger and you welcomed me (Matthew 25.35) . . . By a bow of the head or by a complete prostration of the body, Christ is to be adored because he is indeed welcomed in them . . . Great care and concern are to be shown in receiving poor people and pilgrims, because in them more particularly Christ is received.

In the gateway of Sodom

A second story of strangers and hospitality follows hard on the heels of Genesis 18. The beginning of Genesis 19 finds Abraham's nephew Lot sitting in the entrance or 'gate' of the city of Sodom (just as Abraham had been at the entrance of his tent) in the evening. Like Abraham, Lot greets the two angels (now explicitly identified as 'angels' rather than 'men') with honour, bowing his face to the ground. It is not clear whether Lot was alone at the gate – the traditional place for the conduct of the business of a city – but there is no suggestion that any others responded to the arrival of the visitors. Again like Abraham, he offers them hospitality, inviting them to his home for a meal and a bed for the night. Initially the angels reject his offer but when Lot presses them they accept.

At one level this story is Abraham's hospitality story all over again. There is a significant difference, however. Abraham's life was agrarian and nomadic; he made his home in a tent. Lot, on the other hand, had chosen city life and he lived in a walled city alongside many others. The context in which Lot was offering hospitality was different in that he was offering strangers overnight protection inside the city walls that otherwise would have protected the citizens of Sodom from such strangers. Lot was working within a different, corporate, code of hospitality, in which city walls protected populations from potentially violent strangers, so long as the gates were properly guarded.

Lot's foray into hospitality Does Not Go Well. After a simple evening meal Lot finds his home surrounded by angry and apparently lustful men – all the men of the city. The men demand that Lot bring out his visitors in order that they might 'know' them. Lot refuses, begging the men not to act so wickedly. He offers the men his own daughters 'who have not known a man', saying, 'do to them as you please; only do nothing to these men, for they have come under the shelter of my roof' (Genesis 19.8). This story is often read as one that illustrates God's opposition to homosexuality. The primary issue being addressed here, however, is hospitality – specifically Lot's hospitality to the two strangers and the inhospitality of the residents of Sodom. The clue is to be found in the response of the men of Sodom: 'This fellow came here as an alien, and he would play the judge! Now we will deal worse with you than with them' (Genesis 19.9).

The important word here is 'alien'. The men are angry because Lot is an outsider, yet has taken it upon himself to bring two strangers within the safety of the city walls overnight, thereby potentially endangering all the residents of Sodom. As citizens they would have considered it their responsibility, and their privilege, to decide who would be offered refuge within the walls, and Lot has either usurped them in this role, or shown them up. Biblical scholar Lyn Bechtel has argued persuasively that when the men say they want to 'know' the two strangers in Genesis 19.5 they are using the word 'know' in its legal or judicial rather than its sexual sense. In other words, they want to investigate the men to see whether Lot has exposed them and their women and children to danger by sheltering these two strangers within the walls overnight. On this reading, Lot misunderstands the men, perhaps wilfully, when he offers his virgin daughters in place of the two angels. Lot's offer is grotesquely comic – it underlines his commitment to the responsibility he has taken for the safety of the strangers in offering them hospitality. The responsibility of hospitality, Lot's shocking gesture suggests, is so sacrosanct as to mean that care for visitors is more important than care for one's own children.

The comically grotesque hospitality of Lot is held up in the story against the equally comically grotesque inhospitality of the citizens of Sodom. To some extent, it might be appropriate to have some sympathy for the men of Sodom. They feel that a newcomer has thwarted them in their role of protecting their families and their city. Nevertheless, their expression of their frustration is out of all proportion – as is, of course, Lot's expression of his sense of responsibility toward his guests.

'This fellow came here as an alien'

The two stories of hospitality to strangers, then, deal with different circumstances and with different codes. The story of Abraham's hospitality in Genesis 18 concerns the code by which an individual might offer hospitality to strangers, while the story of Lot's hospitality in Genesis 19 concerns a different set of behavioural norms that come into play when an offer of hospitality is properly a corporate gesture (like today's decisions on the part of states about the acceptance of refugees and other immigrants, for example). Lot's 'crime' was to attempt to take on the role of a citizen when his status was merely that of alien.

The Hebrew word translated here as 'alien' is *ger* (*gerim* in the plural), a significant word in the Old Testament, encompassing a rich range of meaning. Indeed, it appears that the meaning of the word changed and developed over time. In essence a *ger* was a 'stranger' or 'sojourner' – someone who was not a citizen but merely a resident, even though he or she may have been living as a *ger* in a particular place for many years. In earlier times *gerim* were prohibited from owning land and so were invariably poor and vulnerable. The classic group of people deserving of charity, attested especially in Deuteronomy, comprised the alien (*ger*), the orphan and the widow. So, for example, Deuteronomy 24.21

provides, 'When you gather the grapes of your vineyard, do not glean what is left; it shall be for the alien [*ger*], the orphan, and the widow.' Later traditions, such as the holiness legislation of Leviticus, appear to reflect a social order in which *gerim* could own land and slaves and become people of substance to whom Israelites might potentially become indebted. Leviticus makes provision for the *ger* in a different way from Deuteronomy. Instead of categorizing the *ger* as a person deserving of charity, Leviticus 17—26 provides that the *ger* should be treated as if he were a citizen. So, for example, Leviticus 24.22 provides: 'You shall have one law for the alien [*ger*] and for the citizen; for I am the LORD your God.'

The citizens of Sodom class Lot as an alien (*ger*), but that is not the only instance in Genesis in which Abraham and his extended family are described as aliens. Indeed, 'alien' is an epithet used of Abraham and his sons and nephew repeatedly. Abraham is, of course, himself an outsider – Genesis 11 and 12 tell of his journey from Ur of the Chaldeans (in modern-day Iraq), via the town of Haran, to Canaan. Genesis 12 goes on to tell of a famine in Canaan that causes Abraham (Abram) to go down to Egypt and live there as an alien. More surprisingly, Abraham is referred to again as an alien once he has returned to Canaan and even in the context of God's gift of Canaan to him. In Genesis 17.8 God says to Abraham, 'And I will give to you, and to your off-spring after you, the land where you are now an alien [*ger*], all the land of Canaan, for a perpetual holding; and I will be their God.' It seems that Abraham and his family do not lose their status as *gerim* even once the land gift has been made. So in Genesis 28.4 Isaac blesses Jacob with these words,

'May he give to you the blessing of Abraham, to you and to your offspring with you, so that you may take possession of the land where you now live as an alien – land that God gave to Abraham.' What this blessing seems to imply is that even though God had given the land to Abraham, Jacob was nevertheless living in it as a *ger*.

In Genesis 23, in which Abraham approaches the Hittites among whom he lives to purchase a plot of land for a burial place for Sarah, Abraham describes himself as a *ger*. Abraham says to the Hittites in Genesis 23.4, 'I am a stranger [*ger*] and an alien [*toshab*, meaning tenant, plural *toshabim*] residing among you; give me property among you for a burying-place, so that I may bury my dead out of my sight.' His self-description resonates strongly with a verse in the holiness legislation of Leviticus (25.23): 'The land shall not be sold in perpetuity, for the land is mine; with me you are but aliens [*gerim*] and tenants [*toshabim*].' This verse is at the centre of the way Leviticus and other biblical books or passages that scholars describe as 'priestly' understand land and its ownership. For these biblical materials, land belongs to God, so people can never 'own' it as such, but may only be aliens and tenants in it. This appears to be also the understanding of the 'priestly' parts of Genesis (and perhaps also some other parts of Genesis that have not traditionally been understood to be priestly), in which Abraham and his family are repeatedly described as aliens (*gerim*), despite being given the land as a gift by God.

In thinking about Abraham and his family as 'aliens' it is helpful to compare their way of living with the way of living of the Israelites in Exodus and the books following it. In

Exodus God recognizes that his people, the Israelites, are suffering in slavery in Egypt and he saves them, bringing them out of Egypt and into a new promised land. Along the way God gives his people the Torah at Mount Sinai, which includes instructions for what the people are to do when they arrive at the promised land. In short, they are instructed to expel all the original inhabitants of the land so that they can enjoy peaceful and sole possession of it. The books of Joshua and Judges tell the story of the 'conquest' and its qualified success. Central to the understanding of this tradition is the idea that God gave the land of Canaan to the Israelites for their exclusive possession (even if the Israelites had to do the expelling first). The exodus narrative is a wonderful story of salvation that has inspired oppressed peoples, in both ancient and recent times, and has been the foundation for black and other salvation theologies. However, when you read the story through to the end, and particularly if you try to read the conquest narratives from the point of view of the Canaanites(!), it becomes apparent that this is an 'exclusivist' story in which the salvation of God's chosen people is won, to some extent, at the expense of others (and this pattern, too, has been played out in the stories of South Africa, the United States and modern-day Israel, for example).

Abraham's story is different. Yes, he also starts out as an outsider, coming to Canaan from another land, and yes, he is also promised that Canaan will be God's gift to him. However, he comes to a land that is already populated – 'At that time the Canaanites were in the land' (Genesis 12.6) – and rather than try to oust the original inhabitants Abraham sets about the task of becoming their neighbour. He doesn't always get it right, but he lives alongside others and at a number of points he is shown to be concerned about his neighbours' interests, such as when he intercedes for the people of Sodom in Genesis 18.22–33. Indeed, one of God's promises to him is that he and his offspring will be a blessing to other peoples or nations (Genesis 12.3; 18.18; 22.18; 26.4; 28:14). The stories suggest that Abraham is made a sort of 'mediator' or 'conduit' of blessing between God and non-Israelites. He is also identified as an interceding prophet, both implicitly (in Genesis 18.17–19) and explicitly (in Genesis 20.7), and it is striking that Abraham's intercession is always for non-Israelites. In this regard Abraham is unlike both Moses and David, who also intercede but only ever for their own people.

Abraham's is therefore more of an 'inclusivist' story, in the sense that he aspires to live in God's land alongside its other inhabitants, rather than to have exclusive possession of it. Even the language used in relation to the gift of land in Genesis reflects this. The land promise texts in Genesis tend to use the Hebrew word *achuzzah* to signify 'possession' of land. This 'priestly' word is like the old-fashioned English word 'usufruct' and signifies the right to 'use' or 'enjoy' property belonging to somebody else (in this case God). The word used for 'possession' in the books relating to the exodus and conquest tends to be *nachlah*, which has more of an exclusivist sense, even though it also includes the ultimate ownership of the land in God's hands.

The concept of 'stranger' or 'alien', then, has a double significance in the Abraham stories. Not only does Abraham offer hospitality to strangers, he is also called by God to be a 'stranger' or 'alien', living in the land God is giving to him, but alongside others who already belong there. Interestingly, the Rule of Benedict also reflects this ideal from Genesis. As already noted, the rule instructs Benedictines to greet guests as though they are Christ, reminding them that Christ is particularly present in guests who are poor or on pilgrimage. The rule also requires Benedictine nuns and monks to live as though they, too, are guests in their own monasteries. In other words, Benedictines are not to become too comfortable in the occupancy of their own 'home', but to understand themselves to be there only at God's invitation and at his pleasure.

Welcoming the stranger – being the stranger

One must always be cautious when seeking to apply biblical ethics to the issues and situations of today. This is doubly so when the source is biblical narrative. Just a few moments spent pondering Margaret Atwood's dystopian novel *The Handmaid's Tale*, recently and chillingly dramatized for television, will serve to remind us of the potential dangers inherent in a too-literal appropriation of principles from the pages of Genesis. Atwood paints a future world in which procreation has become both difficult and revered, so that the entire machinery of a totalitarian state is built around Genesis's imperative to 'be fruitful and multiply', with horrifying results. Abraham's world and ours are extraordinarily different, but even so, may this ancient story contain wisdom and guidance for our own?

Genesis 18 highlights the generosity of Abraham's hospitality, even to unknown visitors. The treatment of the story here brings to the fore the fact that in Abraham's world he would have been called on over and over again to respond to strangers in essentially similar circumstances. On those other occasions his visitors would not have been divine in quite such a literal sense as his Genesis 18 visitors, yet the story suggests that when we offer hospitality to strangers we too encounter God in our guests. We offer hospitality not because we are looking to benefit in some calculated way, but because to do so is civilized and kind. Nevertheless, one of the ways in which we encounter God in our lives is through meeting other people, and in particular through responding to the needs of people in vulnerable circumstances. We may find, the story suggests, that the gift we receive is greater than that which we give.

Our own culture does not have a comparable set of hospitality codes. It is not that we are not hospitable – it is abundantly clear that many good and generous people in our communities live by well-defined patterns of hospitality – but we lack a common shared code that gives us all a sense that we understand the rules and know how to respond when called on to follow them. This lack of shared expectations and responsibilities makes both the offering and receiving of hospitality more difficult in our context.

If this is true for individuals it is even more true for organizations, like families or businesses, churches or nations. It is the lack of commonly held expectations of hospitality that has nation states tying themselves up in knots over the issue of immigration. My own native homeland of Australia, for example, is a nation of 'boat people' hell-bent on preventing others from arriving by boat. Australia has been so busy 'stopping the boats' and trying, for political purposes, to stem all arrivals of asylum seekers by sea that it has not stopped to think about its proper responsibilities as a citizen nation of a world beset by war, famine and climate change. If Australia was to be ultimately successful in 'stopping the boats', who else might be called upon to take them? The problem is far bigger than it can sometimes seem in any one national context. If larger, wealthier nations do not take their share of the responsibility for responding to this rapidly growing problem, who will?

I should be clear that the stories of the hospitality of Abraham and Lot in Genesis 18 and 19 ought not to be read as suggesting that we, either individually or corporately, should offer hospitality indiscriminately to any person presenting themselves. The Gospels suggest that even Jesus sometimes experienced the needs of the people he encountered as overwhelming (Matthew 14.13–21; Mark 6.30–44; Luke 9.10–17; John 6.1–14) or competing (Matthew 9.18–26; Mark 5.21–43; Luke 8.40–56). Equally, no one nation can resolve the immigration crisis alone. Genesis is not blind to the consequences and the price of offering hospitality to the stranger. That begins to be apparent already in Lot's story in Genesis 19, but a real, albeit brutal, account of the tensions that can arise and grow when strangers dwell in proximity to one another is to be found in Genesis 34's account of the sexual assault of Dinah, Jacob's daughter, and the responses of Dinah's firebrand brothers and her more cautious father.

Yet, despite this level of realism, Genesis depicts God calling his very first chosen family to live as strangers, in proximity to others. Abraham and Sarah and their children are called to live as aliens and therefore to participate and share not in the privilege or security of the citizen but in the vulnerability and uncertainty of the non-citizen. What might our communities or our nations look like if you and I were to think of ourselves as aliens? How might that self-descriptor influence our attitudes, our prejudices and our comfortable senses of identity and entitlement? How might a more widely based adoption of the identity of 'alien' affect the ways in which we, individually or corporately as a nation, look outwards to the needs of others? What impact might it have upon our practice of hospitality and how might that, in turn, affect our propensity to 'let mutual love continue' and, therefore, to find ourselves entertaining angels unawares?

7

Loving your neighbour as yourself

Shulamit Ambalu

Who is my neighbour? This might be the most important question at the heart of the parable of the Good Samaritan. But I will begin with the question that Jesus himself first asks the legal expert in his reply to the original question: how to enter into eternal life.

What is in the Torah? What is your reading of it?

Every writer in this volume is, in some way, entering the core dialogue that structures this parable. As a Jewish writer, however, I begin by engaging with the actual texts and reading traditions that Jesus and the legal thinker both also knew. The parable itself, after all, is in part a critical reflection on the tradition to which I belong. This means that at the outset I am in the position of 'neighbour' in relation to the other contributors to this volume.[1]

This chapter explores the core texts that form a foundation to this parable, and we will discover what they themselves may have to say to us about who our neighbour is. We will see that the answers emerge not only from the words on the page, but in how the Torah speaks and who is being spoken to. We will discover in this language the covenantal source of freedom that gifts us our capacity to respond to our neighbour. We will explore the parallel thinking of the twentieth-century philosopher Emmanuel Levinas, and confront the painful reality that exists in the contrast between our responsibility for our neighbour and our fear. Finally, we see that we will find a liveable ethic in the spaces we choose to enter within our own freedom, and in the active will to balance ourselves between two core imperatives: 'You shall love your neighbour as yourself' and 'Thou shalt not kill'.

When the legal expert approaches Jesus, to test him, and asks how he might enter eternal life, Jesus answers his question with even better ones.

> What is in the Torah? How do you read it?

The legal expert's answer is to both of the questions. His very reply, his choice of words, reveals both his content knowledge and his reading of Torah.

> You shall love the Eternal your God with all your heart and all your soul and all your strength and all your mind, and your neighbour as yourself.

He is speaking words that Jesus of course knows. And both of them know that he is creatively intertwining two core commandments that share the same powerful opening verb, 'you shall love'.

The first part of his reply is a quotation from the Shema, probably recited as a core part of daily prayer in the time that Jesus lived, and more certainly by the time that the Gospels were written down.

And you shall love the Eternal your God with all your heart and all your soul and all your strength.

(Deuteronomy 6.5)

Note that he adds the clause 'and all your mind', an allusion perhaps to how he is using his own mind in his creative response to Jesus' question, and perhaps also to how much he values the life of the mind in his quest for meaning.

The second part of his response cites this central ethical obligation:

You shall love your neighbour as yourself.

(Leviticus 19.18)

He does not include this second verse's opening word, 'you shall love', in his response, because both he and Jesus know that it is there. But by leaving it out, he is in fact creating a deep parallel between the commandments to love God and to love your neighbour. Whenever we, and they, quote from the Torah, they and we are both affirming that quotation in its original place, and at the same time investing it with new meaning. This is a sort of double knowing. A Jewish response to the question, 'Who is my neighbour?' must therefore begin with an understanding of what Jesus and the legal expert knew when they had this challenging conversation.

You shall love your neighbour as yourself.

This stark imperative appears in the Holiness Code, the priestly composition that lies at the centre of the book of Leviticus and also of the whole of the five books of Moses – the Torah that is read in synagogues throughout the cycle of the year. The Hebrew Bible doesn't just carry meaning in its words and sentences. Meaning is also created in the shaping of the text, in the placement of each pericope, in the coupling of verses. It is therefore absolutely significant that this section of Leviticus and this particular verse within it are literally so central to the Torah; one might even say, at its heart.

But can *love* be an ethical demand? This question might and should stop us in our tracks. It is a question that becomes more complicated still by the demand that the love we must show for our neighbour should match the love we feel for ourselves.

> You shall love your neighbour as yourself.
> *V'ahavta l'reacha k'mocha.*

This stark imperative is densely knitted into a matrix of ethical commandments across three verses in Leviticus (19.16–18) that work together to describe who the neighbour is for us, and what we are for her or for him. We will see here that this section is in fact a literary unit, with close links between the word 'neighbour' in the opening and closing verses, linked with the expression 'I am God'.

> You shall not go about as a tale bearer among your people, do not stand by the blood of your neighbour, I am God. Do not hate your brother in your heart; you shall surely rebuke your kinfolk, and do not suffer sin on his account. Do not avenge, do not bear any grudge against the children of your people, but you shall love your neighbour as yourself, I am God.

This relationship with the neighbour is not insipid. It is not driven by a desire to 'help' the other. We see here instead the intertwining of speech and action: the powerful demand to be responsible for that neighbour's very life. Destructive speech (tale bearing) is juxtaposed with the image of one who stands idly by his or her neighbour's blood. Here is the incredible, powerful and deeply challenging command to resist the desire for silence in the face of hating the other: 'Do not hate your brother in your heart.' Instead, you shall 'surely rebuke' your neighbour. In Hebrew, *hocheach tochiach*, the double form of this verb, is a grammatical device that expresses the absoluteness of this imperative; the duty to speak out is unavoidable, because to do otherwise would mean being somehow complicit in that person's sin. This power of speaking must replace the desire for vengeance and enmity; it is the route, the signpost to love. The Torah here rejects the power of hatred to pour out as unmediated emotion into this world, choosing instead the path of confrontation through speaking. Yet in recognizing how powerful these drives are, the wish to stand idly by our neighbour's blood, the secret comfort of hating that person in our heart, the wish for vengeance, this text also speaks to the reality of being human. I believe that it is profoundly true that rebuke, challenge, disagreement and argument are part of that ethical relationship that we also call 'love'.

Both verses are punctuated by a deep and causal meaning: we must do this because this is what God demands of us. 'I am God.' Perhaps this divine punctuation is all the more necessary because the demand is so very difficult.

Who is my neighbour? We have seen something of *what* our neighbour might demand of us, but not *who* our neighbour is. Having looked *in* to the core space in Leviticus that frames this demand, we now take a step *back*. We begin to see a pattern that is so pervasive, so core to the underlying structure, so deeply part of the language in relation to our neighbour, that we can even fail to recognize what it is. Consider these examples.

From Leviticus's Holiness Code:

> Do not defraud your neighbour, or rob; the wages of [your] hired labourer shall not be left with you until the morning. (Leviticus 19.13)

From the Ten Commandments:

> You shall not bear false witness against your neighbour.

> Do not envy/desire the house of your neighbour, your neighbour's wife, his man or maidservant, his ox, his ass, or anything that is your neighbour's. (Exodus 20.16–17)

And from Exodus's Covenant Code:

> If you take your neighbour's cloak as a pledge [against a loan] you must return it to him by sundown. For this is his only covering for his skin, what will he lie down in? And if he cries out to me, I will hear, because I am gracious. (Exodus 22.26–27)

This is only a small selection of examples of commandments referring to our neighbour, but what they have in common with each other and many other examples in the Torah is the sense of *who* is being spoken to. The 'you' here, the person the Torah is addressing, is in a position of some power, of some potential freedom to act towards the other. We might call this a relational power. The person God is speaking to has a duty towards his or her neighbour because the relationship itself is a carrier of obligation. These are all highly specific examples of human interaction, and each commandment addresses the party who holds *more* power. He is the one who hires a worker, or who takes a cloak as a pledge. Both are males here, reflecting the reality of biblical patriarchy, but the address to men also includes women. The tenth commandment, in directly addressing the literal patriarch, is also both specific and general. It addresses the male household head, but this negative commandment, this 'you shall not', clearly addresses everyone. No human being may stand idly by their neighbour's blood; every person must choose the act of speaking in rebuke over retaliatory violence. There is no escaping the reality of social position and gender, but the deeper assumption here is that the Torah is speaking to the person who holds some power; they are in some position of relative freedom.

We begin to see that our neighbour is the other who has a claim on us. God insists, through the Torah, on a conscious limit to the uses of power. It is an insistence that grows out, in my Jewish tradition, of *the* foundational relationship, one that patterns every other: the covenant between the people Israel and God. A people who are partners both as members of this collective and also as individuals, who have the necessary freedom to refuse or choose it. A freedom God creates in us. Since this covenant assumes mutuality, if not exactly equal mutual obligations, then the Torah is assuming this freedom in us. Understood through the lens of the Torah, *every* human relationship has the potential to be modelled upon this pattern; every human relationship should carry a fragment of this covenant within it.

The 'you' to whom God speaks in the Torah experiences a freedom freighted with responsibility; what the great twentieth-century Jewish philosopher Emmanuel Levinas calls 'difficult freedom'. And because the Torah contains a multiplicity of single specific commandments, its message is that there is always more to do. Always another and another obligation. This is obligation born out of our foundational freedom. This very freedom, though, raises a difficult question. What happens when I am utterly power-less? What if I have nothing to offer my neighbour? What becomes of our power to act when we ourselves become the objects of hatred, the ones who are feared, the targets of terror? Can I, must I, hold this complex ethical obligation towards someone who wants to kill me?

The French philosopher Emmanuel Levinas's work is so use-ful to us because he sites his ethics within human relation-ships, within the response to another person as wholly other. That person's other-ness, their alterity, is not a challenge, not 'allergic'. On the contrary, if I am able to see that person's unknowable wholeness, their vulnerability, what he calls their 'face', then I can only respond completely to that person's needs.

> The first word of the face is 'thou shalt not kill'. It is an order. There is a commandment in the appearance of the face, as if a master spoke to me. However, at

the same time, the face of the other is destitute; it is the poor for whom I can do all and to whom I owe all.[2]

Like the Torah, Levinas addresses the reader as one who has the capacity to act in freedom. This capacity opens the way to being able to apprehend the other's face. For Levinas, this is an absolute and unidirectional responsibility.

The first word of the face is 'thou shalt not kill'.

Killing here might mean literal violence, but it also means the act of denying another person's entire and unknowable subjectivity, themselves in themselves, through the assumption that I might 'know' that person. Martin Buber would have described this as an I–It and not an I–Thou relation.

The face of the other commands me; it is destitute.

As in the Torah, the relationship is structured by power and vulnerability. We sense a compelling practical duty calling out to us, growing out of these very words on the page. In my responsibility for the other, I become myself. This is the place of ultimate potential. But the potential may also be reversed.

The first word of the face is 'thou shalt not kill'.

What happens when it is the other who wishes to kill? Is this one too my neighbour?

This is not a theoretical question. Is the rapist my neighbour? The racist? Is the anti-Semite my neighbour? Were the Nazis my neighbours? These questions are not rhetorical. The Jewish experience, if it can be fully heard, and not, as it so often is, labelled and rejected, has everything to teach about the reality of our neighbour. Living at the nexus of difference, between religion, ethnicity and peoplehood, Jews 'catch' and contain the projections of others, while at the same time living actively each in our different ways, to find the fit between different facets of identity; as living in connection with both our specific and richly laden Jewish meanings and our reality as citizen insiders. We have lifetimes of experience both in being the neighbour and of asking who our neighbour is. In these particular times, for example, our experiences teach us to view what we are calling Brexit as a brutal attempt to tear us from our European neighbours, and to dismantle a hard-built peace, an evolving democracy that was built so painstakingly after the Second World War. Peace and democracy consciously built not on the exigencies of trade, but on shared ideals. We see the attempt to dismantle these ideals happening in tandem with the increase in right-wing extremist violence – a violence that even led to the murder of Jo Cox, a Member of Parliament, democratically elected, and known for the way that she lived her life in direct expression of her ideals. Is this politically inspired killer my neighbour?

In these times, when social forces as well as individual people are trying to teach us to fear our neighbour, I must keep my neighbour's face in sight, in spite of the unpredictable random violence that threatens to sweep us up. I must find the language to speak of political–religious–jihadist violence, just as I have seen my Muslim neighbours' own struggle to name and describe the strand of political–

theological extremism that they also reject, and that threatens us all.

I say this as someone whose own neighbour disappeared in Afghanistan; barely out of childhood, this young man on jihad.

I live in the inner city. As neighbourhoods go, this one is relatively quiet, but we have lived through unspeakable violence. A black teenager, brimming with promise, stabbed in the park. Another, a victim of black-on-black crime, killed with a knife. His memorial, flowers changed almost weekly by his grieving mother, tied to a lamp post on my street. Alongside this sense of grief, and our growing sense of insecurity, I genuinely lack the words to fully describe how much my real-life neighbours actually enrich me, and how much we (I believe it is we) give each other in this face-to-face sense of our difference. It is a difficulty that gifts us so much life. I say this emphatically as a Jew in a neighbourhood with almost no other Jews, and as part of a lesbian couple; two women who after 27 years *as a couple* must look carefully all around us each time we even *think* of holding hands on the street, to see if we are safe. Every time. I know the vulnerability of which Levinas speaks.

The first word of the face is 'thou shalt not kill'.

This is the counter-commandment to 'you shall love your neighbour as yourself'. This imperative, 'Thou shalt not kill', speaks to me in a double address. I must not kill, in all the rich meanings that Levinas brings to that word. And I am not obliged to allow another person to murder me. That very vulnerability that I may see in the face of the other is a vulnerability that also belongs to me. 'Thou shalt not kill' means that I am not obliged to permit my own killing. The death, sudden or slow, of my body, myself, my soul. My self-respect. My capacity for an upright way of life. The Torah teaches that almost every other commandment may be set aside in order to save a life. These two core imperatives each provide a ledge for me to stand upon. 'Thou shalt not kill': 'You shall love your neighbour as yourself.'

This must be a complex daily effort. If I am not prepared to stand idly by my neighbour's blood, then I must choose to act from that very place of freedom that the Torah assumes I have. Finding this freedom may sometimes require a conscious effort of inward movement; finding and claiming this freedom, this potential planted in me by my creator. It is a momentary expression of covenant.

This interior covenantal source of freedom, of potential, towards and in the face of my neighbour, is a way of living within hearing of the Torah itself; it grows out of being able to listen to the potential that is being addressed. Why else did we leave Egypt? Why else did our ancestors struggle through 40 years of wilderness, if not to leave their enslaved selves behind? Why else did idolatry appeal so strongly to those people who longed for the familiar bonds that denied them their difficult freedom?

I discover that there is no other way to face this real becoming without the face of the neighbour, the unknowable other. Can I bear my neighbour's face? Can I see that face, not only when my neighbour is close to me, but also very, very distant: a human being on a fragile boat precarious on the Mediterranean; a hopeful parent waiting among countless others for their turn before the immigration appeal court? And can I choose to see it, that distant face, and in so doing choose that place of freedom?

I would suggest that all of Jewish history teaches me that my life requires it. I have been born, despite everything, in a fortunate place. An accident of birth, this particular citizenship, this particular passport.

'You shall love your neighbour as yourself.' What about *love*? Levinas speaks of our responsibility for the other, but not of *love*. *Can* I love my neighbour as myself? Let us look more closely at the sources of the legal expert's quotations in the parable of the Good Samaritan.

> You shall love the Eternal your God with all your heart . . .
> *V'ahavta et Adonai Eloheicha b'chol l'vavecha.*

> You shall love your neighbour as yourself.
> *V'ahavta l'reacha k'mocha.*

Notice a small grammatical difference: '*V'ahavta et Adonai . . . V'ahavta l'reacha k'mocha*' – two tiny particles that serve to attach the objects of this love. The words for 'love God', *v'ahavta et Adonai*, are attached with the particle *et*, which serves to stick a verb to an object. And in *v'ahavta l'reacha*, the prefix *l'* means 'to' or 'for'. Not 'you shall love your neighbour', then, but 'you shall love *for* your neighbour', or *to* your neighbour. As Nachmanides, one of our greatest medieval commentators, writing in the thirteenth century, teaches, it is humanly impossible to love one's neighbour in the same way as one loves oneself (and, one might add, perhaps not even desirable). The Torah is teaching that one should love *for* one's neighbour what one loves *for* oneself. Nachmanides explains that this means awarding one's neighbour with wealth, possessions, honour, wisdom and knowledge. My own love of neighbour might include freedom from persecution, stability, security, citizenship and an upright way of life.

The language of the Torah and its practical demands are deeply interconnected. We learn that loving our neighbour can only mean loving *for* him or *for* her. It is a different love from love for God. We cannot fully know either – our neighbour or God. We already know this most deeply in our love for those we love the most. We sense that despite the depth of our love, we cannot actually 'know' them, and that loving *for* them means leaving some space in knowing that we cannot know. This is a way towards enabling their full other-ness. Loving *for* our loved ones, our neighbour, must ultimately mean a way of acting from that place of freedom to serve them, to allow the full mystery of their face to both command us and in some way resist us; allowing them to live in their totality and difference, their unique and exceptional otherness, unknowable, mysterious, whole, and capable of compelling us. In contrast, *v'ahavta et Adonai Eloheicha*: and you shall love the Eternal your God, simply to love God. The difference is illuminated, and it is this very difference that enables us to understand our obligations to each more clearly. This is intuitively correct. I cannot imagine loving anything for God; what we call love is absolutely never about knowing, and is ever beyond me.

Perhaps this unknowing might support an ethics that acknowledges uncertainty, one that is based on two very certain principles. You shall love your neighbour as yourself. Thou shalt not kill. My uncertainty is in knowing, at any particular time, how to find the balance between them, but my certainty is in knowing that both are fundamental truths. In practice, this capacity for love, and for responsibility for my neighbour, is a choice that can be practised in the search for my difficult freedom. This is a starting place, a core ethical stance. Yet this place of freedom also reminds and requires me to seek my own life, to neither kill nor be killed, and to understand the fundamental limits of my own power, my times of powerlessness. Denying my own power is a deep abnegation of my global and personal responsibility, but denying my powerlessness is a rejection of what is all too real. I believe that it is in the movement between these two core positions, and the movement inwards, in search of our potential freedom, that we may free ourselves of some of the fear of the other, and meet within ourselves the source of power to act.

Notes

1 I am grateful to Dr Ruth Sheldon for this insight.
2 Emmanuel Levinas, *Ethics and Infinity: Conversations with Philippe Nemo* (Pittsburgh, PA: Duquesnes University Press, 1985), p. 89.

8

My neighbour and the ecological crisis

Michael Northcott

I saw flashing lights on the night of the 2016 UK European Union Referendum. I was speaking at a conference on wonder and the natural world at the University of Indiana's Bloomington campus. After an early supper I walked across their very green campus to an Olympic-sized outdoor swimming pool and enjoyed a refreshing swim in the 32°C heat. I walked back to my hotel as night fell, and I began to see flashing lights on the grass and in the shrubs around me. I knew immediately these were fireflies, having seen them in Malaysia where I had taught in a seminary in the 1980s as a USPG mission priest. I had not expected to see them in Indiana, and it was a magical moment. With the afterglow of a long swim and the surprising beauty of some of God's myriad creatures I felt precisely that state of nature-inspired wonder that we had been talking about in the conference hall.

Fireflies are winged beetles. The scientific name of the species family is *Lampyridae* and their female offspring are commonly called glow-worms. They particularly like marshy areas and wetlands, and they glow in the dark to attract partners. One of the chemicals that enables the females to glow to attract mates tastes horrible to predators, so they associate the light with a bad experience and stay away.

But fireflies themselves do sometimes eat each other! The process by which they glow is called bioluminescence, which is a reaction between enzymes in their bodies and oxygen in the atmosphere. In Malaysia fireflies synchronize their flashes so that, for example, at Kuala Selangor, near Kuala Lumpur where I used to live, it is possible to see an amazing synchronous display of flashing lights on the river at night. However, their numbers are declining, in Malaysia, in the USA and around the world, because of the draining of their habitat for agriculture and development, and because of the pesticides that are used extensively in food production.

In Britain, glow-worms are found in marshy and wetland areas in southern England, though they are fewer in number, of course, than in warmer places such as Indiana or Malaysia. However, a number of glow-worm walks are organized, brought together on the website of the UK Glow Worm Survey Home Page.[1] Among the sightings nearest to St Martin-in-the-Fields listed on the glow-worm blog are Happy Valley, Coulsdon in Surrey, and Hadleigh Downs in Essex.[2]

In his opening chapter Rowan Williams says that what we call 'the environment' includes myriad creatures to whom we should be neighbours, just as the Samaritan became a neighbour to the man caught among thieves. As the Samaritan gave life to the one who was robbed, we are called as human beings, and as children of God and members of the body of Christ, to give life to, and sustain, God's wondrous creation.

When you live in the tropics you tend to find that your house contains neighbours you are not very keen to share it with, or give life to. Cockroaches in Kuala Lumpur are far more common than fireflies. They live in the drains and the surroundings of your house, and they will frequently try to move 'upstairs' into your home. In the UK, if environmental inspectors find them in restaurant kitchens, the restaurant owners receive a public health warning. Cockroaches spread disease, and so you are desirous of keeping them out of your house, particularly when you have young children. So yes, I regularly used a pesticide in our drains to keep them as much as possible out of our home. I did not give life to them. I concentrated more on giving life to my children, on sleeping peacefully at night, and having a clean kitchen.

In my cottage garden in Dumfriesshire I have come to love and appreciate insects more than I did in Malaysia. When I pick our autumn raspberries I compete with bluebottles and wasps and raspberry mites. Some fruit I just leave to the insects if they have already started on them. Those insects are useful to us as gardeners. They are part of a whole chain of life, from the biota in the soil, which we have worked strenuously over some years to improve, to the bugs in our compost heaps, to the birds over our acre – including swifts, swallows, robins and tits that eat midges and other insects in turn. We grow our food and flowers entirely organically, without using pesticides or herbicides. That plot of land gives us life, as we have worked to give it life, and to increase the variety of creatures that live there, including the hedgehog that hibernated last winter in the flower border, the butterflies and moths we often see, and the partridges and red grouse that drop in from the Duke of Buccleuch's surrounding grouse moor in order to escape from the bankers and stockbrokers who come to shoot them.

A retired friend stayed with me at the cottage a few months ago, riding up from Newcastle on his motorbike, which has one of those large Perspex windscreens. While admiring the butterflies in the garden, he commented that he has noticed in the last couple of years that he rarely has to stop to clean off the insects from his windscreen – once a frequent occurrence – there just aren't any out there any more.

The marine biologist Rachel Carson awoke my generation to the dangers of herbicides and pesticides in her book *Silent Spring*. Carson combined natural science and romanticism in a powerful narrative that sparked the modern environmental movement in the United States, which spread to Europe and beyond.[3] Carson was dying of breast cancer when she wrote the book. She also testified to Congress about the human as well as ecological effects of the widespread spraying of agrochemicals such as DDT, which was then to be found in the milk of breastfeeding mothers as they consumed pesticide residues in food and water. Pesticides and herbicides intervene at the microbial level of enzymes, hormones and electrical signals between cells, disrupting the electromagnetic forces and signalling systems that give and sustain life. But we too are bodies, organisms, who are sustained by those same microbial signalling systems. And when nervous system and hormone disruptors get into our bodies they affect evolved mechanisms that give life, control organ functioning, and suppress cancers.[4] And hence, as agrochemical use increases not only are we getting silent springs, summers and autumns, as 'the song of the bird is silenced in the sedge', as John Keats put it in the poem apocalyptically evoked in Carson's title *Silent Spring*,[5] we are also seeing epidemics of cancers, and nervous system and gastrointestinal disorders.[6]

The European Union has for some years been trying to establish a system of control of chemical and climate pollution which, until we formally leave, we in the UK are subject to. A few years ago a chemical certification system called REACH was introduced, designed to reduce the deployment of dangerous synthetic chemicals in the environment.[7] The EU recently considered scientific evidence that glyphosate, one of the most widely used herbicides, is a carcinogen, and announced plans to review its use.[8] The EU also banned nicotinoid pesticides because they cause the collapse of bee colonies – though the UK government resists the ban – and led international talks on climate change to restrain greenhouse gas emissions. And France, one of the two founders of the original European Coal and Steel Community formed after the Second World War to prevent France and Germany going to war again over the coal fields on their border, played a key role in the diplomacy that led to the Paris Agreement on climate change in 2015.

But on the night of the EU referendum, as the results came in, first from Sunderland and then from all over England and Wales, it became clear to me before I went to sleep on that night in Bloomington when I saw the fireflies, that this whole raft of environmental protection, along with the protection of peace in Europe for which the EU has stood in its various incarnations since 1948, was in jeopardy, at least for us in the UK, and possibly beyond, as the ripples of the populist anti-establishment vote of that referendum spread across the continent.

And the vote against Europe is not the only straw in the anti-regulatory wind. Environment ministers have since 2010 offered up the largest cuts to the austerity chancellor George Osborne of all government departments. Owen Patterson, and Theresa May's appointee Angela Leadsom, have even expressed doubts – though they have no scientific training – that extreme weather, flash floods, strengthening storms, rising temperatures and melting ice have anything to do with human pollution of the atmosphere. I was told by a senior civil servant that the cuts to the Environment Agency are so great that it will be able to do little more in the future other than intervene when emergencies arise, in the form of flooding, or plagues.

Even if there were any doubt about the human influence on the climate, there is no doubt that agrochemicals are killing off the birds and bees and the microbiota in the soil, and wrecking the broader ecology and creaturely diversity of this sceptred isle. Bird numbers – including life-enhancing birds such as nightingales and owls, as well as cute ones like puffins and tits – are in freefall because the creatures they eat and the hedgerows and wastes where those insects live are being sprayed and ploughed under.[9] But while agrochemicals and heavier tractors and ploughs have given us ever-cheaper food, there are now foodbanks all over our land providing for people on low incomes or those targeted for welfare sanctions who cannot afford to feed themselves and their children.

The people who voted to leave Europe had read for months that the cause of the scarcity of goods and services for people in the UK is immigrants from Europe. They were fed this line in British newspapers, mostly owned either by the Australian businessman Rupert Murdoch or by Jonathan

Harmsworth, IVth Viscount Rothermere and owner of the business that publishes the *Daily Mail*. Harmsworth, like his father Lord Rothermere, loves Britain so much that he lives overseas for much of the year so as to be non-domiciled for tax purposes.[10]

In the North East there is another cause, arguably a deeper one, for resentment against those the people may perceive as the ruling classes of Brussels and London. Coal mines, chemical plants, shipyards, steel works, tank and munitions factories – which were all still producing when I lived there in the 1970s – have been closed in the last 30 years, and products once made or mined on Tyneside, Teesside and Wearside are now imported from Europe and further afield. Male unemployment in County Durham remains scandalously high, with rates of over 50 per cent in former coal-mining communities. Little was done to reskill the people and restore a functioning economy in the North East. And after the visceral civil war that occurred during the miners' strike, when working people were violently set upon by mounted police at pre-planned events, such as the picket at the Orgreave coke works, these communities have been left out of the growing wealth and prosperity that EU and global trade have brought, most of all to London and the south-east of England, since 1979.

While some of us might not have expected a Conservative government to put right the wrongs that came from the collapse of manufacturing and mining industries in the north of Britain, we might have assumed that a Labour government, with its origins in the Methodist and Christian socialist traditions of the late nineteenth century, in power from

1997 to 2010, might have done something about it, particularly with a prime minister whose constituency was in the North East. But despite the considerable achievements of the Blair years – not least the Good Friday agreement, the minimum wage and devolution – the drift of the UK towards growing inequality between rich and poor, south and north, since the neoliberal economic revolution of the 1980s was not reversed. Instead, Blair opened up the UK more fully to immigration from the EU than did our European neighbours, while failing to introduce properly funded adult skills retraining, apprenticeship and small business training schemes for the native population, without which the North East could not recover.

The first Brexit, as I often remind people, took place in 1535 when Henry VIII, having failed to settle his argument with the Vatican, proclaimed himself the head of the Church of England. Since the Synod of Whitby in 664, and much later the Norman Conquest, most of Britain had been part of the Holy Roman Empire. Two-thirds of its arable lands in those centuries had been gifted by farmers and landowners to religious houses, a number of which belonged to the Cistercian order, whose mother house was in France. The English Reformation Henry VIII inaugurated included a large-scale land-grab by the Crown. Thomas Cromwell and his henchmen travelled the length and breadth of England, sacking abbeys, libraries, priories and religious houses, turfing monks and nuns out of their homes, and destroying a centuries-old social order, and along with it 90 per cent of the art in the churches and religious houses. The true Cromwell is as far distant in historical reality from the fictional hero of Hilary Mantel's *Wolf Hall* as it is possible for a novelistic character to be without completely destroying any semblance of historical veracity.

Along with destruction, there was what Marxists call primitive accumulation. The dissolution of the monasteries presaged a wave of land seizures by the Crown and English aristocrats, and was followed in the succeeding 300 years by numerous Acts of Enclosure, passed in a parliament of landowners ironically known as the House of Commons. Thousands of yeoman farmers and their families were evicted from their heritable land rights in a process of environmental and social exclusion which forced hundreds of thousands into the kind of life-destroying vagrancy so powerfully displayed in one of Thomas Hardy's beautiful novelistic elegies for what England had done and was doing to itself – *Tess of the D'Urbervilles.*

England was the first country in Europe to destroy the guild, merchant and yeoman-led economy that had grown up alongside the monasteries in the middle ages, and gradually introduced social protection and customary regulation of land ownership, craft work and trade. As Hilaire Belloc argues in *The Servile State*, the idea of Christian freedom was enshrined in the guild regulation, just wages, just prices and distributed use rights to land and environmental services that arose in England in the middle ages.[11] But even as slavery declined and propertied economic freedom grew in England, so too was propertied freedom's early modern erosion begun in this island, first by the Crown and landowners, then, from the nineteenth century, by the state and state-licensed business corporations. As the Hungarian economist Karl Polanyi wrote during the Second World War,

England led the way in the 'Great Transformation' that turned people into rented labour, or 'human resources', and land into rental value; hence, nineteenth-century England laid the historical and cultural foundation of what we call capitalism. The laws and policies of those who are leading Whitehall's Brexit project offer no evidence that the North East will experience greater economic justice, or environmental protection, from a post-Brexit settlement. On the contrary, Whitehall, Conservative ministers, and much of Her Majesty's loyal opposition, intend to lead this country into a post-EU 'promised land' of *laissez-faire* free trade. In Brexitland, regulations to protect human well-being and ecosystemic health will be repealed, and businesses will be 'free' to turn British people back into corporate serfs, as the mainly foreign corporations that own and run most of Britain's infrastructure, manufacturing capacity and services will no longer be regulated by the European Court of Justice, if Prime Minister Theresa May gets her way.

I return again to Rowan Williams' deeply theological words about global neighbours. He argues that the Samaritan became a neighbour by being a life-giver, and in giving life he received life, as do we when we do likewise. And one of the key things about the parable from the point of view of our global neighbours, and especially the scapegoating of migrants by tax-evading media owners, and the tragic onset of xenophobic attacks and threats throughout Britain after the EU referendum, is that the parable gradually changed in Christendom the concept of moral duty. In classical Greece, and in the Roman Empire, duties both legal and moral were owed between citizens – in the main, Mediterranean males – and to a lesser extent such duties were owed to the families of citizens – their wives and children and slaves. But when it came to foreigners, or barbarians, on the edge of empire, including Palestinian Jews, decimation was their first experience of incorporation and occupation. In the region of the Ten Towns, where Jesus is said to have encountered the woman at the well, the male populace had lost one in ten of its number, and those made landless by Roman taxes had been forced into prostitution or pig-keeping by their Roman occupiers (John 4.1–32).

The Samaritan was a traveller in a foreign country, on the road from Jerusalem to Jericho, and was therefore presumably on a journey home, returning to his own people. But on the road he encountered a stranger, a Jew, who had been robbed and left for dead by thieves; unlike two religious Jews who had 'walked by on the other side', the Samaritan rescued him and gave him life. The parable gradually transformed the definition of moral duty in Western philosophy from fellow citizen, and family member, to a duty of care towards people who are none of these. And so there exists, enshrined in European law, a duty to prevent harm; this was upheld in a French court by a judge who quoted the parable of the Good Samaritan in the case of a motorway driver charged with negligence for having driven past an accident when he could have stopped, at least to call an ambulance, and possibly give aid.[12] We call this in the UK and USA tort law, or third-party responsibility. John Grisham has grown rich writing racy legal thrillers about it, such as *The Pelican Brief*, in which pelican habitat is at issue, not just duties to other persons.

Christian ethics is in essence not about law but about love. The Samaritan did not have a legal duty to follow the law of Moses from the perspective of Christ's audience, since he was not a Jew. But he followed it out of compassion, from the heart, and not from compulsion. Studies of young children by social psychologists show that before they go to nursery or start school, children have innate desires to right perceived unfairness, and prevent harm to strangers.[13] Analogously, children are born with a deep capacity for wonder at the beauty and diversity of God's glorious creation. Sadly, over time and through education and television, or through deprivation of encounters with people from other cultures, or with non-human creatures and the environment, these soulful characteristics of love for all humans and creatures may be gradually suppressed.

That we are evolved and formed as persons to love nature as well as to love other persons ought not to surprise us. There are cultural and spiritual as well as ecological powers at work in the natural environment that is our human neighbourhood and whose non-human inhabitants are our fellow residents. As Christians we believe that these powers stem from the divine origination and sustaining of this world in its beauty and flourishing. Therefore, as Pope Francis argues in his encyclical *Laudato Si: On Care for Our Common Home*, we ought to order our human affairs in this God-made and God-sustained world in ways that follow and underwrite the biological laws that describe its flourishing, including the ways in which we make and procure goods and services. But, as Pope Francis also argues, the tendency of the current form of capitalism, with its idolatry of money, and the raising of the rule of the magic of the market over lawful and moral governance, is to impose forms of land management and kinds of manufacture and trade that are primarily devoted to the law of price, and run counter to moral law and to the laws of nature.

We humans are earthbound souls in our three, or four, score years and ten. I believe, as did some classical Greek philosophers and some Christian theologians, that our souls come from other worlds even more beautiful, fecund and full of a multiplicity of life forms than this one. But in our journeys on earth we build up defences, both cultural and technological, against other creatures, other persons, that we need to train ourselves out of if we are to recover ways of living in this world that will ensure its continuing goodness and fertility, before we pass on, or return, to another world. This is what is sometimes called the work of love.

For all of us, whatever our living arrangements, the foundational context of formation in love is living with and nurturing other family members. Another key context is being in relation with our neighbours in local communities of places. Such relations include human associations to which we belong, such as church congregations and neighbourhood associations. Another context is the communities of species among which we play and recreate in our local natural environments. For many of us, another part of our formation as Christians and persons involves spending time outside of familial and familiar environments, working in other countries, spending time with people from other cultures, learning other languages. These are all ways in which we learn that we are called not only to give and receive love to English people, or to English crops, but to love *being*, and *beings* as our neighbours. And through these experiences, and through the study of science or reading our newspapers, we will have been made aware that when we Christians say we belong to one another, this is a global and not just a local declaration.

Last week I had the privilege of meeting Church of Scotland mission partners visiting from Kerala, South India, Ghana and Zimbabwe. They showed us the already life-threatening effects of climate change and extreme weather on their neighbours, human and non-human. At one of the conferences the visitors addressed, a householder from Inverurie spoke about the traumatic effects of flooding on those whose homes were inundated in her Aberdeenshire community. Thankfully no one died in the floods, and homes were mostly repaired with insurance pay-outs. But in the developing world, climate change is already threatening human life. Extreme weather events are destroying traditional seasonal patterns of food growing, forcing families into urban vagrancy and extreme poverty, and provoking civil wars – such as the terrible war in Syria and ongoing unrest in Ethiopia and Eritrea – that are driving millions on to the roads and seas in search of refuge.

Hundreds of children from climate-damaged regions who have relatives in the UK are at all kinds of risk in the so-called jungle camp in Calais. They are our global neighbours, forced on to our doorstep by the ecological crisis. As a people, as a nation, we would be enhanced by giving them life, and were we to give them hospitality, and the opportunity to make a living, they would no doubt join many other migrants and refugees who have come to this island and who now care for people in hospitals and nursing homes, or work in the construction, hospitality and horticultural sectors, or contribute key skills and know-how in our universities and industries.

Love is not a zero-sum game – quite the opposite. Like the bioluminescence of the fireflies flashing synchronously on marshlands in Malaysia, love for the stranger and for nature, when it is honoured and copied, sustains a larger shared pattern of charity and virtue.

Like that great Londoner William Blake, I like to imagine that the child Jesus of Nazareth visited this sceptred isle with his tin mine-owning uncle Joseph of Arimathea in Cornwall and Glastonbury. I like to imagine as well that the Incarnation can still inspire British people to love their land and her myriad creatures, and inspire them to continue to welcome those not from here. For there is no doubt that this land contains more than enough of God's bountiful provision to sustain natives and refugees alike, provided this island's wealth is shared more equitably.

Notes

1 <www.glowworms.org.uk> accessed 10 October 2016.
2 <http://ukglowworms.blogspot.com> accessed 14 July 2017.
3 Rachel Carson, *Silent Spring*, New York: Houghton and Mifflin, 1962.
4 Theo Colborn, Dianne Dumanowski and John Peterson Myers, *Our Stolen Future: Are We Threatening our Fertility, Intelligence, and Survival? A Scientific Detective Story*, London: Abacus, 1997.
5 John Keats, 'La belle dame sans merci', cited in Carson, *Silent Spring*, p. iv.
6 David Servan-Schreiber, 'We can stop the cancer epidemic', *New York Times*, 19 September 2008.

7 Christina Ruden and Sven Ove Hansson, 'Registration, Evaluation, and Authorization of Chemicals (REACH) is but the first step – how far will it take us? Six further steps to improve the European chemicals legislation', *Environmental Health Perspectives* 118 (2010), pp. 6–10.

8 Erik Stockstad, 'Why Europe may ban the most popular weed killer in the world', *Science*, 17 June 2016 <www.sciencemag.org/news/2016/06/why-europe-may-ban-most-popular-weed-killer-world>.

9 Norman McLean (ed.), *Silent Summer: The State of Wildlife in Britain and Ireland*, with foreword by David Attenborough, Cambridge: Cambridge University Press, 2010.

10 'List of people with non-domiciled status in the UK' <https://en.wikipedia.org/wiki/List_of_people_with_non-domiciled_status_in_the_UK> accessed 13 July 2017.

11 Hilaire Belloc, *The Servile State*, London: T. N. Foulis, 1912.

12 Zen Bankowski, 'How does it feel to be on your own? The person in the sight of autopoesis', *Ratio Juris* 7 (1994), pp. 254–66.

13 Felix Warneken and Michael Tomasello, 'Altruistic helping in human infants and young chimpanzees', *Science* 311 (2006), pp. 1301–3.

9

My neighbour the refugee

Sarah Teather

Rowan Williams opens this book with a question that has struck me before about the parable of the Good Samaritan. The lawyer poses a question – who is my neighbour? Why doesn't Jesus answer it straightforwardly? To an extent in these encounters I often think he doesn't answer the question – and his capacity to get away with that is something, as a former politician, I can only marvel at. Not only does he not answer it, but more than that, Luke's very framing of the encounter makes it clear that the question itself is problematic. The lawyer is not seeking the truth but trying to justify himself. He is being a smart alec, testing Jesus out. As Rowan goes on to point out, Jesus' answer does not really provide us with a neat formulaic solution for who should and should not deserve our charity. Instead he seems to turn the question on its head.

The question of who does and does not deserve our resources is one that haunts public discourse in respect of migration and refugees. As the crisis in response to refugees arriving in Europe (and I do usually refer to it as a crisis about refugees not a refugee crisis) reached its noisiest point in 2015, there were frenetic attempts to choose and select, divide and label, so as to avoid any duty or obligation to those arriving in need. Were they economic migrants or refugees?

Syrian refugees, people say, might be worthy of our charity, but Africans? This suspicious and censorious division was reflected in politicians', as well as wider public, discourse. Theresa May, at that point Home Secretary, sought to distinguish between those we choose to resettle from the camps and those who seek entry under their own steam. She made out that asylum seekers are queue-jumping, chancing it. They should wait in line.

This is a world-view that is framed by a model of scarcity – our scarce resources, their extreme need. I don't deny that there is need or that meeting it can be challenging, but if that is our only prism for viewing the world it can be pretty limiting; and I am not convinced it chimes with the parable of the Good Samaritan.

The concept of 'neighbour', on which the parable turns, recurs throughout the Bible. Why is it so important? I asked Nick King SJ, Scripture scholar, who has recently done a new translation of the Bible. 'What did neighbour mean to the people of Genesis and Leviticus?' I asked. 'How did people live? What did it look like? I have a picture of what a neighbour is now, but what about then?' He reminded me that some people would have been nomadic. This struck me. Many of the early figures of the Bible spent much of their lives on the move, on a journey. Seen in this light, the image of a neighbour is not simply a static one. It centrally designates someone who is passing close by, who is arriving or has arrived from elsewhere. 'What about the word used for neighbour, then? Can you tell me more about that, the linguistic connotations of it?' Patiently Nick went through all the mentions of neighbour in Hebrew. The word used is

Reh', which literally means another, close by, as you would expect. But it can also mean friend. Indeed, the word implies some level of reciprocity to the relationship. It isn't quite as simple as just being the object of a duty.

There is something else more interesting to me. The same word is used to describe Moses meeting and talking to God in the tent in Exodus, where it says, God spoke to Moses 'as one speaks to a friend' (Exodus 33.11). The same word gets used to describe basic rules that govern social interactions between people in early Jewish society, but also to describe a sacred meeting face to face with the source of life.

Neighbour God. I couldn't quite get the thought out of my head and wondered why it felt so familiar. Then I remembered Rainer Maria Rilke's extraordinary poem of the same name from *The Book of Hours*.

> You, neighbor god, if sometimes in the night
> I rouse you with loud knocking, I do so
> only because I seldom hear you breathe
> and know: you are alone.
> And should you need a drink, no one is there
> to reach it to you, groping in the dark.
> Always I hearken. Give but a small sign.
> I am quite near.
>
> Between us there is but a narrow wall,
> and by sheer chance; for it would take
> merely a call from your lips or from mine
> to break it down,
> and that without a sound.

The wall is builded of your images.

They stand before you hiding you like names.
And when the light within me blazes high
that in my inmost soul I know you by,
the radiance is squandered on their frames.

And then my senses, which too soon grow lame,
exiled from you, must go their homeless ways.

Rilke had a complex relationship with faith, rejecting his Catholicism;[1] nevertheless, his attempt to turn standard concepts of God upside down captures something interesting. Rilke's neighbour God is vulnerable, alone, thirsty, groping in the dark. But the poem is intimate – seeking, knocking, listening for breathing – so close, so near, yet separated by a wall. A wall 'builded of your images'. A wall between neighbours that condemns them both to exile, homelessness, as the longing for relationship is squandered on the frame of names. Images can indeed build walls between us human beings – and *therefore* between us and God.

A wall 'builded of your images'. What image do you have of a refugee? What comes to mind first when you hear the word? Images from TV screens perhaps? Huddled masses, hauled from freezing water, traipsing across muddy fields, queuing at hastily erected border fences, jostling with police lines, crying children. People fleeing from war – whose images are also seared into view. Destruction, dust, disaster, bloodied children pulled from rubble. Such images of trauma and human need provoke intense emotions in most of us if we are really honest with ourselves: fear, panic and hostility mingle with pity, compassion and connection. They mingle with other images and names too – like 'illegal immigrants' with its linguistic connotations of criminality. Images of Muslim refugees are overladen with images of violence and the name of Da'esh. The wall is builded of your images and the light is squandered on the frame of names.

After leaving Parliament and before joining the UK office of the Jesuit Refugee Service (JRS), I spent some months with the international JRS office as a kind of itinerant member of the advocacy team. This meant that I met a lot of teams in the field and visited some of the key pressure points across Europe. I walked with groups of refugees across the border from Greece to Macedonia on the route so many were using to cross Europe. It was unlike any other experience I have had with JRS. People had such a sense of purpose – it was hard not to be swept up in it. I had learnt a few phrases of Arabic – only enough for introductions and broken conversation. But it was enough to catch glimpses of people's lives. There was the little boy I shook hands with in Greece with his granddad from Aleppo. The old man with the dodgy hip who struggled on the rocky road and had to be helped up on to a car by Red Cross workers, still smiling and laughing. The young man who had carried his wounded brother for most of the journey – he had lost his legs in a bomb in Syria. His eyes were red with tiredness, but on he went. And the little girl aged around nine who shared my first name, with all her belongings in a yellow carrier bag. They are just fragments, but they are etched on to my memory.

Even these should not be the only images that inform our understanding of the refugee. We need a fuller picture because, even if authentic, an isolated image is easily distorted when placed among other, false, images. There is a risk that images of Syrian refugees dominate so much that we miss the fact that they are not the only refugees on the move. Iraqis and Afghans were also significantly represented in those knocking at Europe's door in 2015. But there are other, hidden refugee conflicts we see less of: Burundi, South Sudan, CAR – crises JRS is responding to around the world. There are also many West Africans, who perhaps first migrated to Libya for work but then were forced to leave when Libya collapsed. In the chaos that followed our military intervention in Libya, many were imprisoned and tortured and so in desperation made the dangerous journey over sea to south Italy. Eritreans are fleeing forced conscription and human rights abuses too.

In the UK, we receive asylum applications from all of the above and more besides – DRC, Iran, Pakistan, Uganda, to name but a few. Amid the UK's notoriously hostile public discourse, images of where an acceptable refugee comes from cloud the application process, reducing the chances that these applications will receive a fair hearing. So too do images of the scale of immigration. The scale of the sudden influx of people to Europe in recent years is like nothing we have seen for decades, but it is still as nothing compared with the numbers of refugees accepted by Lebanon and Turkey from Syria, or Uganda from South Sudan. Most of those fleeing conflict seek help first from their near neighbours. The UK received just 37,000 asylum applicants in 2015. Compare that with 1.25 million into Germany, for example. It is a drop in the ocean. But the false image looms so large in our minds that it obscures the reality.

In Britain, these toxic images pervading public conversation are not the only walls that segregate refugees from wider British communities. The government also actively builds walls to stop people from helping one another. At JRS UK, we have a special ministry to work for those who are detained or made destitute as a result of government policy. By destitute I mean forbidden from working, forbidden from claiming benefits, now even forbidden from lodging with friends who rent for fear of falling foul of the right-to-rent rules.[2] We have accompanied people over the last few years who have been kept in detention for years and others who cycle in and out of detention. The impact on their mental health is significant.

At JRS, we want to break down both of these mutually supporting walls – the one built of false images, and the one built of hostile government policies. We are mindful that the names used to describe people can build walls, and so we refer to refugees who seek our help not as customers or clients but as friends. And we actively seek to get to know people, to know them by name. At our day centre, we talk to people about their Home Office case, but we also talk about other things, like their children, the news, politics, football; we share stories of our week with one another. It is in accompanying in this way that we learn the detail of what it is to live in the shadows – to need to move from friend to friend, hoping not to outstay a welcome, or to spend the night in the all-night McDonald's or on night buses. But the image of a refugee in need gets flushed out by other, more complex pictures – of resilience and humour, of skills unused, of hopes and dreams, of a liking for tomatoes or cheese or a particular turn of phrase. We speak to one another as friends.

There is a certain cost in that, as it means we are emotionally engaged with the story – the ups and downs of the Home Office saga, the failures of the lawyer, the failing health that complicates the picture. I know that one woman I usually have lunch with in the day centre is currently sleeping on the floor because her mattress is worn out, and she hasn't been able to visit her family for some time. I think about it. But it is also true that if I go into the office overburdened, it is usually our refugee friends who notice. And I notice when one of the friends I know by name is not there. Friends and neighbours do things for one another. Neighbourliness and friendship are indeed reciprocal, not one-sided.

An important context to this is the extraordinary mix of people. Our staff and volunteers are a mix of lay and religious, Jesuits and sisters of different orders, and many refugees. Some of our refugee volunteers have their papers, and are able to work, but they choose to volunteer to give something back. But many others don't have their papers. They live in uncertainty and limbo, but still choose to give generously of their skills, supporting other members of this diverse community from other walks of life.

When one of our refugee friends learnt what we were spending on sandwiches at the day centre, he was so outraged by the cost that he offered to cook hot food for all our day centre guests for free. He has no immigration status, but he is a trained chef. He cooks with enthusiasm and love and has since been joined by another refugee volunteer who alternates efficient cooking with warmth and pastoral care for others in the day centre. We give out small amounts of cash to our refugee friends to enable them to get to solicitors' appointments and the like. One of our volunteers who helps run the travel money desk has no money herself, but she gives her skills to the task with generosity.

The contribution of refugee volunteers is like an engine that drives our work – an energy unleashed in the building of skills untapped and joy unmined. Their generosity is the glue in the relationships in the building. They are neighbours to us and to other refugees whom they would never have met had they not journeyed, or had they chosen to keep their gifts hidden or unshared. The refugees who volunteer may be materially poor but they bring a richness that is difficult to measure.

Rowan Williams in his chapter notes that Jesus turned the legislative question of who I owe a duty to on its head, maintaining that the neighbour is the surprising stranger who can save your life; so surprising that you need to keep a certain openness to neighbourliness if you are to spot these life-giving encounters – encounters to be found on the road. The surprising stranger may, as in the parable, be a foreigner – the hated Samaritan, whose very name evokes disdain. The neighbour may, as in Rilke's poem, be vulnerable, thirsty, alone – yet still be where we find the God of life.

For is it conceivable that, as Sam Wells suggests in his book *A Nazareth Manifesto*, the parable of the Good Samaritan is not a story of duties and rules, but one about Jesus himself?[3] Is the hated foreigner actually the Lord of life? The one we can't accept help from because we have 'builded' walls of their image and framed them with the names we give them? Frames that deflect the light inside us and the light that we seek – the intimacy with God that we long for, knocking, seeking? For isn't the neighbour, as I found in my hunt through the Hebrew text, not just a word for our duties, but the possibility of a sacred meeting face to face? Neighbour-friend, meeting with the Lord of life?

If we frame our relationship with refugees only in images of their need and our scarce resources, we miss something important. But if we approach them as friend, we find that their truth and ours is much richer. This is the truth that religious communities and parishes have found who have been hosting our refugee friends through our At Home scheme, who had many anxieties initially about how they would cope with the need (and make no mistake, some placements have been stretching); but all have found that their experience of hosting has brought new life to the community that they could not have foreseen. Unexpected friendships have blossomed, such as that between a guest and an elderly religious everyone thought was cranky. The laughter and vitality changed the whole community.

Seen in this light, the refugee images the Good Samaritan, and similarly the God who meets us as a friend and neighbour in the incarnate Christ. The refugee is not the one we must confine to legalistic categories of need to preserve our resources, but the one who brings a richness and a gift. Turn the question on its head. Neighbour-friend, sacred meeting face to face.

Notes

1 See e.g. Ralph Freedman, *Life of a Poet: Rainer Maria Rilke* (Evanston: Northwestern Univeristy Press, 1998), pp. 144–5.

2 For more information, see the report by the Joint Council for the Welfare of Immigrants, 'Passport Please: The impact of the Right to Rent checks on migrants and ethnic minorities in England' (February 2017): <www.jcwi.org.uk/sites/default/files/2017-02/2017_02_13_JCWI%20Report_Passport%20Please.pdf>.

3 Sam Wells, *A Nazareth Manifesto: Being with God* (Chichester: John Wiley and Sons Ltd, 2015), p. 90.

10

Whatever happened to the common good?

Anna Rowlands

Not long ago I spent a Sunday evening giving a talk in a pub in Sunderland. It wasn't a talk on Brexit, but rather on the core issue that coursed through the veins of the Brexit debate: migration.

The evening's revellers were made up of the local Catholic community, who had issued the invitation for me to speak, members of an Iranian church who turned up in number following their evening service, a group of Nigerian and Indian students and migrant workers and the local Sunderland white working-class men who make up the more typical Sunday evening drinking crowd.

Perched on a stool at the end of the bar, just beneath an enormous screen showing *Britain's Got Talent* for those whose interests quite understandably lay elsewhere, I gave a talk on the way that Catholic social thought provides resources for thinking about the current migrant crisis. It was an evening when I was (unsurprisingly) cheered and heckled in equal measure: political theology as a fittingly extreme sport.

At the end of my talk I suggested to the crowd that rather than a standard question-and-answer session, we would get much more out of the evening if we attempted to have a 'common good conversation' about migration – one in which we attempted to speak and listen with respect to the diversity of views and experiences in the room, searching for a sense of our common humanity and shared interests but aware of the real differences that should not be ignored. If we can't get that right in a pub in Sunderland, who are we to expect our politicians to do any better?

The first contribution came from a middle-aged working-class man who had listened intently to every word of my talk. He spoke at length about his sense of the world. In summary he presented the following case: 'I love people, I'd do anything for anyone, but what's wrong with the world is religion; it births division and evil. And what's wrong with accepting migration is that these migrants are all religious, and mainly Muslim. Syrians or Turks, they are going to bring division. Muslims disapprove of us and of our way of life. How do I make friends with a stranger, a co-worker? I invite them for a drink after work; for working men the pub is the heart of the community: we form bonds by sharing a pint. But my Muslim co-worker won't drink with me, won't do what men around here have always done. It's a way of judging us. I want to live in a real community that works hard and knows its neighbour, where we look out for each other. That's what we used to do around here. But I can't do that with people who are really different from me, with whom I have nothing in common.'

As he was talking, one of the local parishioners, a retired nurse, walked towards the man and put her hand on his shoulder. When he had finished she told him that she shared his sense of the loss of community and that she too wanted Sunderland to be a place of real neighbourliness. But, she explained, her experience of nursing at home and abroad had given her a rather different perspective on religion, on reasons to welcome migrants and ways to build relations with Muslim neighbours. This was the beginning of an exchange more revealing and important than the talk that preceded it.

My Sunderland interlocutor finds his views echoed in much of the Brexit debate. The institutions that were meant to guarantee our common bonds, to ground our common life and to foster a decent life for communities like ours have broken or proved themselves false and fair-weather friends. Migration (real and fictional/anticipated) is indigestible. There is mourning for the loss of 'settled' community. And so, the last utopia for many is not human rights but the nation state. In the face of precariousness and the erosion of communities, the protector of the local and the fragile becomes the national: the nation state as a vehicle for memory and aspiration. Watch the UKIP campaign videos replete with fighter pilots and 1980s cricket heroes if you don't believe me.

Despite collective (cosmopolitan) surprise at the prevalence of such a complex sense of loss and aspiration (I will come back to the aspiration part) there is not much new about this. These are pan-European (now global) trends that Tony Judt, left-wing public intellectual and self-described Euro-pessimist, wrote about two decades ago.[1] He believed that European elites were failing to grasp that the narrative of 'Europe' stood increasingly for the winners, the wealthy regions and sub-regions of existing states. The losers were 'the European "south", the poor, the linguistically, education-ally or culturally disadvantaged, underprivileged, or despised Europeans who don't live in golden triangles along vanished frontiers'. It turns out that much of the post-industrial English North feels rather like the European 'south'.

Judt argues that what is left to such Europeans 'is the nation, or, more specifically nationalism'. He distinguishes between two forms of resurgent European nationalism – one charac-terized by movements for regional separatism in which regional identity operates in association with a larger trans-national unit (think Catalans or, closer to home, Scottish nationalism), and the other based on an appeal to some contemporary version of the nineteenth-century state invoked as a protection against the dislocations brought by globalization. He argued that if the latter trend was left unaddressed the European project would crumble.

What Judt did not foresee was the intense interaction – of action and counter-action – now taking place between such nationalisms: a political stage shared by Nigel Farage and Nicola Sturgeon, as politicians of the so-called 'extreme centre' vanish. Nor did he see the potential for the vast and complex coalition of interests that the Leave vote brought together. Which prophet could?

But Judt did see the real possibility of an emboldening, not so much of a civic nationalism rooted in institutions but of an ethno-nationalism of blood and soil, which appeals to many of those who feel themselves to be outside of – or to despair of – civic institutions. Once emboldened by elite and opportunist political leaders (who understand few of these political undercurrents and are unlikely to be its victims, and whose hubris is to imagine that their leadership will be respected by such groups), this particular breed of nationalism is a truly terrifying force, a sterile and negative political force nonetheless capable of very great harm. The considered political response to the gradual polarization of our political culture was to ask a binary question, and then be pained when the fault lines emerged in sharp relief, and simmering sentiments of racial hatred broke into the open.

Discourses of theodicy, nationalism, pluralism, liberty and globalization are bound tight around each other in the conversation of the post-industrial North East. It is less a question of bringing theological perspectives to bear from the outside than spotting that these are already theo-political conversations in so-called secular spaces. Read the case made by my Sunderland friend again if you aren't sure. As Luke Bretherton argues, this is about theodicy.

For many Labour Leave voters this was the moment when Thatcherism, never voted out of office, was finally given its electoral kicking. For others, their desires were expressed as a vote against more recent immigration, precarious and pointless work, and a visceral desire to kick back against an establishment that appears to despise and humiliate low-wage workers. It was about resisting humiliation and dehumanization. Much of this, of course, has nothing to do with the EU. But that doesn't matter much. It is a judgement on the neo-liberal politics of Blairite Labour as much as on Thatcherism; it's a way to understand what you do with grief.

In the face of this kind of political emotion, the lacklustre Remain campaign focused on jobs and economic security, but it did not connect or inspire with a robust vision of the good, nor did it name the humiliation and dehumanization many feel and seek to explain how a genuine European Union could take this up into its own political core and offer new forms of participation. To rephrase the late Judt, just as an obsession with 'growth' has left a moral vacuum at the heart of some modern nations, so the abstract quality of the idea of Europe presented by Remain proved insufficient. 'The mere objective of unification is not enough to capture the imagination and allegiance of those left behind by change.'

But we make a huge error of judgement if we suppose that these conversations are only motivated by loss or suffering or by a politics of fear or hate. This is to miss at our peril the palpable sense of aspiration addressed by my Sunderland interlocutor and many others like him for certain kinds of common goods – an orientation towards the good of living in a community of people with faces and names, with the possibility of purposeful existences and a desire for a responsive politics, of the desire for a kind of common protective humanity that many now middle-aged working-class communities did not experience in their childhood encounter with religious institutions.

And so any credible Christian theological response that desires to resist and overcome the binary Manichean logic of good and evil so prevalent in our culture needs to handle the presence of a felt sense of both loss and aspiration, suspicion and resilience, betrayal and pride, as Augustine might say – *ad permixtum*. The fault lines of the referendum result run through the human heart, not simply between classes and communities. A Christian metaphysics requires us to handle the complexity of these mixed-up motivations with care.

Pope Francis astutely and disconcertingly notes that a culture in which compassion is absent from politics – for all, not just for our various preferred characters – more likely than not has first experienced a failure of civil society and its intermediate bodies. We stop being properly human with each other in and between our localities first, and then we find we cannot sustain communities of welcome for more distant neighbours whose very lives depend upon it. Brittle and exhausted democracy, a lack of political resilience, a struggle to grasp and respond decisively and with leadership to the duty to near and distant neighbour, the difficulty of talking about the goods rather than interests we want our politics to pursue: all this becomes the thin soup sustaining a weak body politic.

To be clear: there are good reasons for those who voted Remain to grieve, for there are tangible goods that will be lost and it is unclear that we have political mechanisms in place right now to secure our common well-being. But that grief must retain its attachment to its real object: the pursuit of the life of the common good. Our divisions are publicly exposed. There must now be a genuine process of listening beyond silos – and make no mistake, this will be deeply unsettling. What and who (who on earth?) will enable us to recognize the devastation of our political culture – a devastation many years in the making – but do so in such a way that we are also able to recognize the fragile possibility of the new political community that might already be buried alive underneath the rubble? This is ground that a new generation of political and church/religious leaders must speak to: leaders that we are calling forth from where, and how? This is territory wide open for those with ears to hear and eyes to see.

In the pub in Sunderland no great settlement was agreed, no revolution in thought occurred, but at the initiative of a local church stepping beyond its settled ground, a community with firmly held and very different views on immigration was briefly, for a few hours, in fruitful dialogue with itself: a dialogue that was not for its own sake alone in response to the need to discern duties to global neighbours in urgent need.

We need not only new leaders and a commitment to processes of robust, open-hearted dialogue, but also new spaces of civic encounter – new ways to address my interlocutor's question: when money is scarce and civic institutions are largely gone or viewed as irrelevant, where (rather than how) do we form bonds of affection and a sense of shared life across different classes, ethnicities and faiths?

Note

1 Tony Judt, *A Grand Illusion? An Essay on Europe* (New York: Hill and Wang, 1996).

11

A better kind of politics

Brendan Cox

II

A better kind of politics

Brendan Cox

Like it or not, politics affects all of our lives. It affects us personally, making it easier or harder to get a decent job, a home or a good school for our children. It affects the things that we care about, the people we try to serve through our work and the issues that matter to us – poverty, climate change, the safety of the world for us and our families.

Politics should enable us to make choices as communities, cities and countries that create a shared good life despite changing circumstances. It should provide structure and secure boundaries for our lives, yet we all know enough history to know that politics can go horribly wrong. Sometimes this is catastrophic, as in Nazi Germany and Stalin's Russia. More often, politics simply fails to deal with the challenges of the time. This has its own costs – children badly educated, people unnecessarily poor, older people left in inadequate social care.

When politics goes wrong or fails to respond to events, it creates a sense of insecurity and disorder that can quickly get out of control. Failing politics can provide the space for extremism to grow. Absurd ideas can begin to feel like sensible policy to those who believe that the world should be ordered primarily for their benefit. Fear can lead normally rational people to look for simple but false solutions.

We are facing destabilizing change on multiple levels – to the environment, ethnic diversity, changing patterns of work and relationships, and questions over the way the economy is run – combined with widespread powerlessness to change it. Events like the financial crisis and ongoing terror attacks, combined with these ongoing challenges, have led to increasing levels of insecurity and fear. We are forced to ask foundational questions about the way we order our lives and our continued ability to live well together.

The lack of evident solutions to these challenges has created space for populist parties – on both left and right – to offer what look like simple solutions, appealing to nostalgia for a world that once seemed more stable. They divide the world into friends and enemies, and by doing so build a following of devotees but fail to understand or confront the complexities of the world as it is.

Politics ought to help us answer these questions, yet at the same time as we face these challenges we have become sceptical about the ability of both the state and market to best order society to everyone's benefit.[1] Both concentrate power in institutions beyond the reach of most of us: government, the civil service or boardroom. Outside of the state and market many of us have lost or stopped participating in many of the institutions that used to provide spaces for collective action and deliberation: the Church, trade union or working club.

The result is too often a sense of powerlessness. We can respond by burying our heads in the sand, hoping that someone else will ride to our rescue. I do not believe that that is the right response. Instead, those of us who still wish to live in a tolerant, open and forward-thinking society, those of us who recognize the scale of the challenges we face but also believe in our collective power to resolve them, need to step forward.

Progress and populism

It wasn't always like this. For most of our lives, Jo and I believed that the world was getting better and that it would continue to do so. It wasn't that either of us felt that progress was inevitable, but we did believe that the world had entered an era when reason was on the march and tolerance and inclusivity were ascendant. Despite its many evident flaws and its tendency at times to generate more heat than light, we believed politics to be one of the best ways to change the world. I still do.

The months before Jo's death began to challenge our belief that things would inevitably improve. Over dinners with friends we began to talk about our fears of growing populism, a coarsening of political debate and the stoking of hatred against minority groups. We both began to worry – not about some catastrophic event that would change everything, but that a series of events, driven by feelings of insecurity and fuelled by demagogues, could create a downward spiral that might get out of control.

We talked about what more we could do to help prevent a slide towards extremism, but we never imagined that political violence would hurt us. Then, on 16 June 2016, Jo was killed. Later in court the suspect said, 'My name is death to traitors, freedom for Britain.'

Members of Parliament don't get murdered in Britain. This horrific event was surely an aberration. Yet it happened in a context that makes such aberrations more likely – one in which posters featuring a picture of Syrian families seeking safety claimed that the country was at 'breaking point'; one in which hatred is routinely whipped up against certain groups, and in which politicians and judges are talked about as enemies of the people.

This is not just a British problem. The rise of the populists and extremists – who tell people that the problems they face are the fault of some other group – is a global phenomenon. Marine Le Pen in France, Viktor Orban in Hungary, Nigel Farage here at home and Donald Trump in the USA have much in common. They share a strategy based on exploiting divisions between people, promoting fear and hatred on the basis of identity.

In America, the election of Trump has at least shattered the collective complacency, but it has also given succour to the extremists who feel empowered to act out their hatred, as we have seen in Charlottesville, with horrific consequences. In Europe, the election of Macron and the failure of Wilders to do as well as feared is lulling elites into a false sense of security that we have turned the corner after a populist blip. In 2017 moderates won in Austria, the Netherlands, France and Germany, but the real story is the far right parties, which did terrifyingly well.

In an age of insecurity and anxiety, tapping into people's desire for group identity is a key component of the appeal of the populists, yet the truth is that we all have multiple layers of identity and belonging. Jo was always comfortable with her multilayered identity. She grew up in the Yorkshire constituency she represented yet she married a man born in Lancashire. She was incredibly proud to be English and British, but she loved her five years living and working in Europe. Jo saw no contradiction between these identities because there is no contradiction.

Questions of identity are too often left to extremists to exploit, as too many of us have felt uncomfortable talking about identity for fear that we might offend or exacerbate racist attitudes. We need to get better at telling our own story and building a stronger and more inclusive set of national and regional identities. A core part of that is to balance talking about our differences with discussing the things that bind us together. If we fail to explain identity, or to define what makes Britain truly Britain, then others will do it for us. This leaves the way open for our identity to be defined in opposition to the identities of others, rather than as a positive vision for who we are.

Critical to this is forging a degree of national consensus on our values and beliefs, but the polarization of our politics makes that harder. US politics should be all the warning we need about what happens when politics becomes partisan and divisive, yet you can see elements of it here. Our politics has become polarized between ardent Leavers and Remainers, or between far left and far right, making it all the harder to address the day-to-day challenges we face in housing, inequality and security, not to mention the more fundamental questions of who we are.

Trust

The challenges in our politics are, I believe, closely related to a crisis of trust. A collapse in trust in our leaders and institutions has got us to a point where people aren't sure which way to turn, not just in the UK but in most of the developed world.

The communications firm Edelman conducts a trust and credibility survey every year. The 2017 survey revealed the largest ever drop in trust across the institutions of government, business, media and NGOs.[2] Government is now the least trusted institution in half of the 28 countries surveyed. Even more worryingly, 53 per cent of respondents believe that the whole system – political, economic, work and education – has failed them, seeing it as unfair and offering little hope for the future. Only 15 per cent believe it is working, while a third are uncertain.

The survey concludes that in the UK we have 'underinvested in the levers of trust across the board', that we are 'experiencing a total collapse in trust in the institutions that shape our society', and that there is 'an unprecedented feeling in the UK that life is not as fair as it used to be'. This is unrelated to income and education – even the rich and well educated are worried. Attitudes for many are no longer defined by left and right, but by a political realignment around those who have 'faith in the system' and those who don't.

This loss of faith hasn't come from nowhere. Some of it has come from specific events like MPs' expenses, the financial crisis and the invasion of Iraq. I believe it is also driven by a growing fear of forces that feel beyond our control – immigration, extremism, the erosion of societal values and the pace of technological change – and a belief that politicians don't have the answers.

Rebuilding trust will need politicians to be honest about the challenges we face and our ability to meet them. It will mean paying attention to the institutions we have and those we are going to need, building anew and rebuilding as we can.

Community

It isn't just elite institutions that are being hollowed out, it's our communities as well. Being socially connected to others is vital for our well-being, but the UK is becoming an increasingly lonely country.[3] Shockingly, we are less likely to have strong friendships or know our neighbours here than in any other country in the EU.[4] This isolation damages our health, employment and life outcomes.[5]

Over two million older people, and 60 per cent of 18–34-year-olds, describe themselves as always or often lonely.[6] Loneliness has thrived as civic associations have declined. The institutions that used to pull us together are increasingly weak or absent, whether the Church, family, pubs, local shops or trade unions. Membership has long been falling, and social connectedness – the bonds of affection that make life worth living – has declined along with them.[7]

These changes are happening for a number of reasons and not all are bad; it's not for me to tell someone to have a faith or to join a trade union.[8] But the point is that the sources of solidarity, affection and communion that gave British communities a sense of shared identity are being eroded, and little is being done to stop it. The result is that we live in increasingly homogenous and often relatively shallow communities, increasingly based on social media rather than in the real world.

I believe that a lot of the problems of our politics – including our inability to understand or value the views of people we disagree with, and people's growing willingness to flee to the false dawns of the far right and the far left – are in part a result of this loss of social connectedness.[9] If we don't know our neighbours, our ability to empathize with them, understand their views or choices and build social solidarity is lost.

The loss of social connectedness has come about in part due to political choices. Inequality has risen dramatically over my lifetime because of choices made by successive governments. This has been shown to damage social connectedness, making it harder to build and maintain bonds across different groups in society.[10] Inequality fuels a sense of unfairness, contributing to a lack of trust in institutions and the system.[11] It makes it harder to create the kind of politics we need to address the challenges we face at home and abroad.

If we want happier, healthier people and communities we should focus a lot more on creating trusting and connected societies. Civic engagement and ties to friends and neighbours can create the happiness equivalent of a doubling of income, both directly and through their impact on health.[12] A growing economy matters but it has to be linked to a sense of fairness if we want it to result in stronger communities as well as a rise in GDP.

The challenges of our time

Our loss of trust in our politicians and institutions and our reduced social connectedness and civic engagement are not just problems in and of themselves. Together they create a context in which we are less able to face and address three linked insecurities that confront us.

Rising economic, physical and cultural insecurities have combined to create a sense of powerlessness and fear for the future. One of the many tragedies of our mainstream politics is that it has failed to even acknowledge, never mind address, these insecurities, leaving the voices of anger and extremism to speak from the side-lines, attracting those most in need of change and a way out.

Economic insecurity has risen as the burden of social risks has been shifted to the individual rather than the state or employer. Think of the shift from long-term employment to the rise in zero hours contracts, or the move from final salary pension schemes to private pensions with little guarantee of future income. Real wages have declined; in fact, the UK is the only large advanced economy that since the financial crisis has seen declining wages paired with a growing economy.[13] The result is that the economic recovery has not been felt by many people, increasing their sense of exclusion and isolation. People have become used to working for low wages with few rights and no guarantee of future work, holiday or sick pay, a pension or a pay rise, with the adverse impacts on mental health, relationships and well-being that you would expect.[14]

Our politics has hardly begun to address the economic insecurity we have now, never mind considering how to respond to changes coming down the line, including automation, artificial intelligence and the consequent loss of jobs and whole sectors of employment. Millions of UK workers are at high risk of being replaced by robots within 15 years as the automation of routine tasks gathers pace, while in the longer term 30 per cent of jobs are under threat from breakthroughs in artificial intelligence.[15]

The idea that each generation will be more fortunate than the last no longer applies and perhaps helps to explain why young people often feel that traditional politics has little to offer them. Even those in graduate jobs increasingly see themselves as unlikely to be able to afford to buy a house – a situation that would have been unthinkable for their parents.[16] For many, their education will be their biggest investment in life, where for their parents it would have been a home, and the education would have come free. The rise of the gig economy is only going to increase intergenerational unfairness; those hiring from online platforms tend to be older and better off, those doing the work younger and poorer.[17]

Recent decades have also seen a rise in physical insecurity – people's fear of extremism and terrorism. Attacks in Europe,

Manchester and London, often involving cars or vans driven into crowded spaces, have made it all the more real. Forty-two per cent of English people say that they are more suspicious of Muslims as a result of the London and Manchester terror attacks.[18] A quarter now believe that Islam is a dangerous religion that incites violence.[19] It's a similar story in the USA: following attacks in 2015, the proportion of people saying that terrorism was the most important issue facing the country rose from 4 per cent to 19 per cent, raising it above any other issue.[20] These fears were stoked by Trump and his team: in his election campaign he called for Muslims to be banned from the USA and declared, 'I think Islam hates us.'[21] In the election his supporters were more than twice as likely as Clinton supporters to have negative views of Islam.[22]

Finally, cultural insecurity has risen because of rapid migration and the fast pace of change. Populist politicians have argued that immigration has happened too quickly, that new arrivals have separated themselves off from the rest of society, and that indigenous cultures are under threat.[23] Regardless of the reality or not of changes in society or immigration as a causal factor, some people do feel powerless in the face of change. There is a sense of 'no one asked us' in relation to high levels of migration in some communities. A lack of GP appointments and available housing may have far more to do with government failure than freedom of movement, but it is understandable that people equate their lack of opportunity or progress with changes in their communities.

With each of these insecurities there is no 'off' switch – no easy option. Blaming foreigners won't solve them; nor will leaving the EU. We need a politics that can face these challenges head on and that is honest in its assessment of the challenges, our possible solutions, and the changes we need to embrace in the way we live and work.

What we can do

So the question is, what can we do about it? If we can't turn off the drivers of insecurity, what action can we take to adjust and still achieve our goal of an open, tolerant, trust-filled and equitable society?

When times are hard the temptation is to blame others before we accept our own responsibility for the politics we have. It is easy to point at elected leaders, or to people who voted for the other team, and think that it's all their fault. A better politics is one where we are all willing to step up – and the nature of this crisis will require it. This means talking to people we don't agree with, not just denouncing their views or hoping that someone else will sort it out.

I think a key part of the answer is to focus back on rebuilding our communities. In doing this we can break down social isolation, improve integration, reduce fear of 'the other', forge a common identity, build trust and increase our resilience in the face of change. At a local level we need to find ways to bring people together. This could be through reinvigorating existing institutions or creating new ones.

At least some of this has to happen offline; social media simply can't provide what real relationship offers. Those of us involved in education need to work to structure our schools and education to bring people together rather than put them in silos based on class, religion or ethnicity. The fact that schools have become more segregated than the communities they are based in is the opposite of what should be happening. We could do the same through the arts, sport, shared workspaces and adult education.

Nationally, if we're dissatisfied with the politics we have it's up to us to work for a better one. More of us committed to a better future need to join political parties, stand for office and campaign for change. In contrast to the ideologically driven and often paranoid politics of the far left and far right, we should do this with an awareness that people we disagree with could have something to teach us, and if we work together we could achieve more. We need the humility to see that we could be wrong; that we don't have a monopoly on wisdom about how to live well.[24] Democratic politics does not begin when the people we disagree with or don't like have been forced to leave the room.[25] Joining in is the first step to changing something important to us, whether as a party member, a charity campaigner, a candidate or something else.

What you can do

It isn't my place to tell the Church or other people of faith what to do. However, I believe passionately that the Church and other faiths have a central role to play in creating both a better politics and communities where space is made to celebrate and renew what we hold in common.

The country is undoubtedly a far more secular place than it was 50 years ago, or even in my childhood. The opportunities that has created for people to make their own choices about how to live, who to love, and what to believe are, I think, mostly welcome. Britain can be an amazing place – where else would you find a capital city with a Muslim mayor as comfortable, and as welcome, at a Ramadan iftar one week and at Pride the next? We really have come a long way.

Despite this, I do not believe that secularization has created a country where the voice of faith communities is any less welcomed or wanted. In a country where politicians are trusted by 21 per cent of people, and business leaders by 35 per cent, the fact that two-thirds of the country trust faith leaders and clergy is astounding.[26] This gives people of faith an opportunity and also a responsibility to speak and to play an active role in society.

In my experience there are two different kinds of faith leaders and members – those who look inwards and those who look outwards. In my view it is those who look outwards who have achieved most and who have embodied the best elements of their traditions. I think of William Wilberforce and his long, finally successful, challenge to the British slave trade, and of Dr Martin Luther King, so central to the civil rights movement and whose speeches and writings were infused with a righteous, biblical anger.

I do not believe that faith is the only motivator for powerful, world-changing political activism, but it is certainly one of them. When faith leaders speak out courageously on issues where we need a moral perspective from someone one step removed from party politics, my experience is that people welcome it. People of faith and no faith want the Church to speak and to act on issues of poverty, justice and fairness. In recent years, for example, the Archbishop of Canterbury's voice has been welcomed on issues including the injustice of payday loans and the plight of refugees. Not everyone is going to agree, but everyone agreeing is not the point.

In part, this welcome is due to the awareness that the Church backs up its words with action; church activity forms a huge part of the estimated £3 billion contributed to the country through faith-based voluntary action. We know that politicians don't have all the answers, and we look for people to enter the debate whose job it is to stand up for the poor, the vulnerable, the people at the bottom of the pile. That voice could be yours.

I know that people can be put off political involvement because they may not understand all the dos and don'ts, or think that they might offend, or that they might not agree with everything that is said. I'd guess that people could have similar thoughts when they consider joining a church.

I think that Jo would ask you to get involved anyway. You don't need to know all the answers. Part of the point of getting involved, after all, is to learn as well as to contribute. There are many ways to get involved – join a party, stand for council or join a local campaign against injustice. You'll find a place to contribute. You might also find yourself challenged.

As for local institutions, I would ask you to embrace your role as centres of community both with your own people and working in partnership with others. One of the many astounding things we were able to celebrate during the Great Get Together weekend, held on the anniversary of Jo's death, was the sight of different faith communities coming together to celebrate what we all hold in common. Some of my favourite events were the Chief Rabbi hosting an interfaith iftar at his home, a Bake Off held between Jewish and Muslim young people in Scotland, and an interfaith meal held in the shadow of Borough Market mere days after the terror attack.

I would encourage you to find ways to honour and celebrate your distinctiveness while also working with others to celebrate and build what we hold in common. Faith institutions can be building blocks of social connectedness in our communities – or they can be isolated islands of people afraid of those around them and afraid of difference. Our country needs you to choose the former. You have a role to play.

Finally, I would encourage those of you who are so good at dealing with the consequences of bad politics – running foodbanks, hosting drop-ins for refugees and asylum seekers, and giving to poor communities overseas – to find ways to address the causes of these failures. Foodbanks are amazing places and the people who run them heroes, but by rights there should be no need for them in a country as rich as our own. Helder Camara famously said that when he fed the poor he was called a saint, yet when he asked why the poor had no food he was called a communist. I don't ask you to be communists, but I do want you to ask why and to look upstream to the source of these injustices. Changing the system can seem harder than plugging the holes, but we need both if change is going to happen. Politics is worth your time.

More in common

Where Jo's death was intended to silence her, it has instead meant that she and all she stood for have found a new voice. Her words have gained a resonance in part because of who she was – someone who really did follow through with action and tenacity – but also because they are more important now than they ever were.

I find that many people deeply believe we have more in common than that which divides us and yet are fearful that this will be taken from us – by extremists, by an economy that drives us apart, or by a pace of change that leaves us feeling powerless or left behind. The loss of social connectedness and the linked challenges of physical, cultural and economic insecurity are real. Together they are damaging our communities and our politics, creating space for extremists and the danger they represent.

Rebuilding our communities and rebuilding our politics from the ground up is not optional, it's imperative. There is, I believe, a huge desire for this; when given the opportunity to reach for something better, people grab it with both hands. The Great Get Together took us aback; we were astounded that so many millions across the country would get involved, hosting over 120,000 events. People want to live life in common and when given the chance will throw themselves into street parties, barbecues and fun runs simply for the joy of doing life together.

I hope that we can find ways to help people come together for more days of fun and celebration of what we have in common, but also for the more serious tasks of bringing peace to our communities, finding ways for us to live well together whatever our background or belief, and renewing our politics to deal with the challenges of our age.

A better kind of politics needs politicians who face the future rather than the past, who seek a renewed economic, physical and cultural security in a world of artificial intelligence, an ageing population, and global migration that is arriving whether we like it or not. Building it will mean us finding ways to step away from the anger and vitriol that has so quickly become commonplace. It will mean finding ways to renew our communities, our civic institutions and our politics at a local level. It will mean us stepping up to campaign for what we believe in, to stand as candidates and to join forces with people we sometimes disagree with.

Jo would have maintained her positive outlook and determination despite all that has happened – not out of mindless optimism, but because she believed that what we hold in common is more significant than our differences. It is our job to realize that vision.

Notes

1 <www.edelman.co.uk/magazine/posts/edelman-trust-barom
   eter-2017-uk-findings/>
2 <www.edelman.co.uk/magazine/posts/edelman-trust-barom
   eter-2017-uk-findings/>
3 <www.huffingtonpost.co.uk/asma-dassu/why-we-all-need-to-
   be-mor_b_12352740.html>

4 <www.independent.co.uk/life-style/health-and-families/features/britain-has-been-voted-the-loneliness-capital-of-europe-so-how-did-we-become-so-isolated-9566617.html>

5 <www.ophi.org.uk/research/missing-dimensions/social-connectedness/>

6 <www.independent.co.uk/life-style/health-and-families/features/britain-has-been-voted-the-loneliness-capital-of-europe-so-how-did-we-become-so-isolated-9566617.html>

7 <www.standard.co.uk/comment/comment/decline-and-fall-of-emotional-and-social-wealth-8736866.html> <http://research briefings.parliament.uk/ResearchBriefing/Summary/SN05125

8 <www.standard.co.uk/comment/comment/decline-and-fall-of-emotional-and-social-wealth-8736866.html>

9 <www.respublica.org.uk/wp-content/uploads/2015/01/Children-and-BS.pdf>

10 <http://blogs.lse.ac.uk/politicsandpolicy/big-society-social-capital/>

11 <www.imf.org/external/pubs/ft/wp/2016/wp16176.pdf>

12 <http://member.iftf.org/node/3941>

13 <www.ft.com/content/83e7e87e-fe64-11e6-96f8-3700c5664d30> <www.manchester.ac.uk/discover/news/having-a-bad-job/>

14 <http://uk.businessinsider.com/job-insecurity-extremism-2017-2?r=US&IR=T>

15 <www.theguardian.com/technology/2017/mar/24/millions-uk-workers-risk-replaced-robots-study-warns>

16 <www.theguardian.com/business/2016/feb/14/economics-viewpoint-baby-boomers-generation-x-generation-rent-gig-economy>

17 <www.theguardian.com/business/2016/feb/14/economics-viewpoint-baby-boomers-generation-x-generation-rent-gig-economy>

18 <http://hopenothate.org.uk/rising-islamophobia-challenge-ahead/>

19 <http://hopenothate.org.uk/rising-islamophobia-challenge-ahead/>
20 <www.nytimes.com/2015/12/11/us/politics/fear-of-terrorism-lifts-donald-trump-in-new-york-times-cbs-poll.html?mcubz=0>
21 <www.cnn.com/2016/03/09/politics/donald-trump-islam-hates-us/>
22 <www.vox.com/2016/9/12/12882796/trump-supporters-racist-deplorables>
23 <www.demos.co.uk/wp-content/uploads/2017/02/Nothing-to-Fear-but-Fear-Itelf-final-short.pdf>
24 <www.abc.net.au/religion/articles/2017/06/29/4693897.htm>
25 <www.abc.net.au/religion/articles/2017/06/29/4693897.htm>
26 <www.independent.co.uk/news/uk/home-news/church-sees-largest-drop-in-public-trust-as-hairdressers-deemed-more-truthful-a6826871.html>

12

My neighbour, God's gift

Samuel Wells

I want you to imagine a series of alternative contexts in which the notion of neighbour arises. You're at home, busy with something important to you, perhaps intensely private, and in any case not to be interrupted, and a person who lives nearby appears at the door, knocking, enquiring, demanding, intruding. Or, there's great news, of the end of a war, or terrible news, of the assassination of a beloved leader, or an unprecedented event, like an earthquake in the home counties or a drastic flood nearby – and one way or another, conventional demarcations and boundaries break down, and you speak to people you'd usually no more than nod to and feel common cause with those who'd previously been more or less strangers. Or again, you're sitting on a train. There's a distressing noise from further up the carriage. A person is holding their head and grimacing, clearly in terrible pain. Something's obviously very wrong and you've no idea what it is, but you feel you have to look, you're impelled to draw near, you have an urge to ask other passengers if they know what's happening or what any of you can do. Or here's one more. You're staying in a friend's house. You're alone, and you're coughing, and it won't stop. It's not a normal cough – you grasp that there's something badly wrong. Your mobile phone doesn't have any reception and you realize you need to find a landline. You can hear music in the flat upstairs. You think, 'I've got to knock on that door.'

I've scattered these scenarios by way of introduction because I want to break the word 'neighbour' down into its different connotations. I've chosen four emotive examples because I want to highlight the disconnection between the benign term 'neighbour' and the degree of anxiety evoked by the question, 'Who is my neighbour?' There are broadly three inferences of the word 'neighbour'. The first is literal: it's the person next to you, usually permanently, in the sense of the one who lives next door, but also momentarily, as in the one who's beside you in the lift or on the bus. The second is rather abstract: it's the sense of neighbour as generalized other, whom you have not chosen but rather, for a longer or shorter time, been given – the work colleague with the unconventional eating habits, the argumentative person in the grocery store, the disconcertingly attractive person sitting next to you in the cinema; but more generally, the vacant lot beside your house, the person you see walking with lots of plastic bags talking to themselves, and, at moments of paralysed compassion, a whole nation in the midst of civil war, a town you see in a television story about a devastating hurricane, or Antarctica as it rapidly loses its icebergs. Most discourse about the word 'neighbour' circles around either these literal or abstract conceptions.

But there's also an emotional pull to the word 'neighbour'. This apparently harmless word evokes a profound, visceral and primal reaction. 'Neighbour' becomes a cipher for 'impossible demand'. We spend our whole lives trying to gain control, to have enough money, enough comfort, enough security, enough trust in the people around us, that we won't be dragged off the rocky boat into the merciless waves. But that's precisely what the neighbour threatens to do: the neighbour is the person who, through intrusion, manipulation, limitless need or infuriating invasion, presents us with impossible demands. And we're divided, our hearts are torn, by the self-preservation and self-assertion that says, 'No, I've tried so hard, for so long, to get to a place of sufficiency: I'm not having this interloper drag me down into the abyss,' and the guilt or compassion that says, 'That's a human being, that's a person who deserves my respect and support. That could easily one day be me – that has, at another time, been me.' And it's that torn, confused heart that the challenge of being a human person in an individualized society is about.

If we look more closely at what lies inside the tangible fear of impossible demand, what do we see? We've already noted the sense that I will lose something. It may be space, it might be freedom, it could be resources, security, safety, or at the very least time, emotional energy, money. That's the force of the word 'demand'. But there's also the word 'impossible'. That's a subtler anxiety. If I'm bringing skills, experience, networks, expertise, I will still, almost inevitably, given the scale and complexity of the demand, fail; and if I'm simply bringing a willing heart and a humble hand (in other words, nothing more or less than myself), I just won't have what's required. Either way, it keys into an underlying fear of emptying out with no replenishment, like a balance sheet haemorrhaging losses or a blood donor giving out more than anyone can afford to lose. Impossible, insatiable demand leads to the overarching sense that this will take more than I've got and the consequent lapse into burnout, failure, exhaustion, depression. For many, the answer to the question, 'Who is my neighbour?' becomes 'the one who promises to drown me in a boundary-less ocean of need'.

Emma Jane Kirby's novel *The Optician of Lampedusa* epitomizes this notion of neighbour. It offers a fictionalized account of the disaster in October 2013 in which 300 migrants, largely from Eritrea and Somalia, died. The nameless (and therefore universalizable) optician lives on the tiny island of Lampedusa (population 6,300), 127 miles south of Sicily and 70 miles from the coast of North Africa. (Lampedusa was the site of Pope Francis's first official visit outside Rome, in July 2013, when he prayed for migrants living and departed and upbraided their traffickers.) Out at sea with eight friends, the optician hears the cries of migrants in the water. Standing on the cabin roof, this is what he sees.

> Bodies were flung like skittles across the sea's glassy surface, some bobbing precariously, some horizontal and horribly heavy . . . Every time a wave collapsed, a black dot or head was revealed. The sea was littered with them . . .

> How, he thought, how do I save them all? He lowered his outstretched arm slowly. In the water, hands stretched despairingly upwards, clutching at air, reaching futilely towards him. He could see yellowing eyes staring wild and wide at him, frantic at the hope of salvation.

> He glanced down at his friends on deck. Eight. There were eight of them and there were scores, no, hundreds

of people in the water. And they had just one rubber ring.

Even before he jumped down from the cabin and back onto the deck, the optician had understood that he would have to choose who would live and who would die.[1]

Kirby's novel identifies precisely the sense of being over-whelmed by need – but also the rewards of doing what one can, and the sense of solidarity established with those with whom one can engage. The strongest sense, nonetheless, is that the optician represents Europe, and those in the water embody an ocean of need.

I'm going to tell two stories that address precisely this pro-found, visceral feeling. The stories don't refute this emotion, nor do they provide a precise alternative answer to our ques-tion. If they do give an answer, it's not precisely the same one. But together I believe that they recast the question in a way that provides us with a different question – one per-haps easier to answer, and more empowering to respond to.

In his 2014 book *Just Mercy: A Story of Justice and Redemption*, Bryan Stevenson, founder and executive director of the Equal Justice Initiative in Montgomery, Alabama, and Professor of Law at New York University Law School, portrays the real-ity of being black in America. Stevenson describes what has shaped the notion of race in the USA.[2] Slavery casts an indescribable shadow. But there's also the reign of terror that pervaded the South from the end of Reconstruction until the Second World War. African Americans hear the talk of the new experience of domestic terrorism after 9/11 and say, 'We grew up with terrorism all the time. The police, the Klan, anybody who was white could terrorize you. We had to worry about bombings and lynchings, racial violence of all kinds.' There were countless ways black people could offend a white person that might endanger their lives.

Stevenson notes how the modern death penalty was created as 'an attempt to redirect the violent energies of lynching while assuring white southerners that black men would still pay the ultimate price' (p. 299). Convict-leasing was a routine method of criminalizing former slaves by convicting them of absurd crimes so that they could be leased to commercial enterprises and effectively forced back into slavery. The successes of the civil rights movement haven't eradicated the legacy of the Jim Crow era of segregation. Stevenson describes how racial profiling works in practice: sitting alone, smartly dressed, in a courtroom, he himself could be told to get out and wait in the hallway until his lawyer arrived, until he politely informed the judge that he was indeed the lawyer. Mass incarceration fits this overall pattern. As Stevenson puts it:

> The extreme overrepresentation of people of color, the disproportionate sentencing of racial minorities, the targeted prosecution of drug crimes in poor communities, the criminalization of new immigrants and undocumented people, the collateral consequences of voter disenfranchisement, and the barriers to re-entry can only be understood through the lens of our racial history. (p. 301)

Stevenson describes how the prison population in the USA has increased from 300,000 in the early 1970s to 2.3 million today. The cost has increased even faster, from $6.9 billion in 1980 to $80 billion today. One in every three black males born in this century is expected to go to jail. A horrifying number of children are incarcerated in adult prisons, in the only country in the world that sentences children to life imprisonment without parole. Over 50 per cent of prisoners have a mental illness, and there are more than three times the number of people with a serious mental illness in prison than there are in hospital (p. 188). And within this system lies a litany of dreadful, damaging, and often deliberate mistakes and miscarriages of justice, together constituting a system that Stevenson describes as being 'defined by error' (p. 16).

The story that forms the backbone of Stevenson's account is that of Walter McMillian, from Monroeville, Alabama. The deepest irony of the story is that Monroeville proudly identified itself as the setting for Harper Lee's 1960 novel, *To Kill a Mockingbird*, an account of a 1930s white lawyer who bravely defended an innocent black man. Not only had Walter McMillian himself never heard of the novel, but the law enforcement officers and justice representatives of the town contrived in Walter's case to subvert every value portrayed in its narrative. Walter started his own pulpwood business, which gave him some economic independence but attracted suspicion from those who believed that undereducated black men should know their place. Once Walter's philandering habits extended to sleeping with a married white woman, he was in danger. When the beautiful young daughter of a respected local white family was murdered, in 1986, and after several months no one had been charged, the county sheriff embarked on an elaborate plan to frame Walter, gaining damaging testimony from people Walter had never met and overlooking the fact that Walter had spent the whole morning of the crime entertaining guests for a fish-fry at his home. Due to the seriousness of the charge, Walter was put on death row even before his trial, one of many illegal and transgressive actions brought to bear against him in the subsequent proceedings. Fifteen months after his arrest, an all-white jury, in the face of overwhelming evidence to the contrary, pronounced Walter guilty, and after they had recommended life imprisonment the judge escalated it to a death sentence.

Bryan Stevenson's organization, the Equal Justice Initiative, has, since its foundation in 1994, saved 125 men from the death penalty. Stevenson tells the story of his struggle for justice through the setbacks and successes of the Walter McMillian case. One evening, Stevenson drove deep into the woods outside Monroeville to a trailer park and was greeted by well over 30 family members who knew that Walter was an unstable husband but found their hearts broken and their standing in the community shattered by the manifest injustice of Walter's impending execution. The whole community was being victimized, and otherwise decent white officials were becoming locked into a narrative of denial, deceit and dishonesty.

Stevenson would see Walter about once a fortnight, and gradually they came to be friends. Walter, it became clear, was a kind, decent man with a generous nature. Stevenson not only enjoyed the friendship: he realized that gaining his client's trust was crucial to winning the case. As he puts it:

> A client's life often depends on his lawyer's ability to create a mitigation narrative that contextualizes his poor

decisions or violent behavior. Uncovering things about someone's background that no one has previously discovered – things that might be hard to discuss but are critically important – requires trust. Getting someone to acknowledge he has been the victim of child sexual abuse, neglect, or abandonment won't happen without the kind of comfort that takes hours and multiple visits to develop. Talking about sports, TV, popular culture, or anything the client wants to discuss is absolutely appropriate to building a relationship that makes effective work possible.

Finally in 1993, through the tireless work of Bryan Stevenson, six years after his trial, and after repeated breakthroughs and devastating setbacks, Walter McMillian was cleared of the charge of murder and released from jail, to a wife who could no longer bear to live with him and a community that felt every scar of what he had endured all those years on death row. Walter and Bryan talked almost daily on the phone as he made tentative steps to re-enter life outside. Walter shared the true depths of the despair he'd experienced watching other prisoners go to their execution. Stevenson earned him some degree of compensation for the injustice he'd suffered, and Walter resumed work cutting timber. But one day Walter was struck by a stray branch that broke his neck. During his long recovery, for two months he lived with Stevenson in Montgomery, 100 miles to the north. For a few years after that Stevenson would take Walter to New York to answer questions in his law class at the university. But in time the effects of the broken neck hastened the onset of dementia, and when Stevenson visited him in a care home, Walter felt as though he was on death row for a second time.

As Bryan looks back on his journey with Walter, which is simply the most poignant and time-consuming of scores of such cases, he asks himself, in a spirit of mystery, why he does what he does. Sitting in tears after putting the phone down on a man who was to be executed later that evening, Bryan looks back on 25 years of struggle against inequality, abusive power, poverty, oppression and injustice, and realizes that he doesn't do what he does because it's required or necessary or important, or because he has no choice. He does it because he is broken too. Exposure to all this hurt and evil has revealed his own brokenness. In the words of Thomas Merton, we are bodies of broken bones. Stevenson believes:

> Being broken is what makes us human . . . Our brokenness is the source of our common humanity, the basis for our shared search for comfort, meaning, and healing. Our shared vulnerability and imperfection nurtures and sustains our capacity for compassion.

> We have a choice. We can embrace our humanness, which means embracing our broken natures and the compassion that remains our best hope for healing. Or we can deny our brokenness, forswear compassion, and, as a result, deny our own humanity.

Stevenson perceives: 'We've thrown away children, discarded the disabled, and sanctioned the imprisonment of the sick and the weak – not because they are a threat to public safety or beyond rehabilitation but because we think it makes us seem tough, less broken.' He recalls victims of violent attacks and relatives of the murdered, 'and how we've pressured them to recycle their pain and anguish and give it back to the offenders we prosecute . . . how we've allowed our victimization to justify the victimization of others. We've submitted to the harsh instinct to crush those among us whose brokenness is most visible.' But so doing simply leaves us all broken. Stevenson recalls from his college days in Philadelphia an old minister who would throw his arms wide as the choir were about to begin, and say, 'Make me to hear joy and gladness, that the bones which thou hast broken may rejoice.' Finally, Stevenson realizes:

> The power of just mercy is that it belongs to the un-deserving. It's when mercy is least expected that it's most potent – strong enough to break the cycle of victimization and victimhood, retribution and suffer-ing. It has the power to heal the psychic harm and injuries that lead to aggression and violence, abuse of power, mass incarceration.

I turn now to a very different kind of story – a novel, by and about a woman, and set in England; it is about suffer-ing but not so much about injustice, and has other perhaps more significant differences that I return to below. Jojo Moyes' novel *Me Before You* tells the story of Louisa Clark.[3] Lou, 26, is devastated when she loses her job at the local café, where her outgoing nature perfectly fits the diverse clientele and makes her feel she has a vital role in the com-munity. Having few qualifications, she has little choice of local jobs, and takes one of the hardest: she becomes carer to Will Traynor, aged 35, who, she discovers, was paralysed when hit by a skidding motorcycle two years earlier.

The job starts badly. She's eager to please, to make tea, to cheer him up, to tidy, cook – whatever it takes to break into the steely gloom of his static negativity. In a pivotal scene, Will receives a visit from Alicia, his girlfriend back at the time of the accident, along with his old London colleague Rupert. It turns out that the two friends are full of dread because they've come to tell Will they've got engaged. Alicia is mortified with guilt, and as she leaves she explains to Lou that she didn't simply abandon Will; she spent months trying to do things for him – but he wouldn't have it and she gave up. After Rupert and Alicia have left, Will manoeuvres his wheelchair to the mantelpiece and uses his stick to sweep to the floor every photograph on display there – many of which are of him with Alicia. Lou spends hours trying to repair the photo frames and restore the pictures to their former glory. Will is furious. He says, 'You wanted to fix what I did yesterday . . . It would be nice, for once, if someone paid attention to what I wanted. Me smashing those photographs was not an accident . . . I don't want to have those bloody pictures staring at me every time I'm stuck in my bed until someone comes and bloody well gets me out again.' To which Lou, provoked, with cheeks aflame and with nothing to lose in the midst of her failure, responds, 'You don't have to behave like an arse' (pp. 73–4).

This confrontation marks a turning point. Thenceforth Lou is more prepared to let Will have some space in his sadness, and Will begins to take Lou seriously as a person in her own right and not just an agent of his family's attempt to mollify his life. Will even allows Lou to cut his unkempt hair and shave his dishevelled beard – a very visible indicator of his emergence from furious depression. It seems that he will let her do some things for him, after all. Encouraged by this, and at a suggestion from her sister, Lou develops a bucket list of things she thinks will help Will engage with the simple joys of living. Her ambitions lead her to take Will and his physiotherapist to the races to enjoy watching and betting on the horses. It turns out to be a desperately unsuccessful expedition, as a mixture of wheelchair-unfriendly facilities, bad luck, and an obstinately miserable Will ruins any sense of adventure and turns it into an afternoon of torture. The day sums up the catalogue of failures and humiliations Lou endures as she tries to rescue Will from his condition – and from himself.

Three further events qualify Lou's sense of what she's trying to achieve. Her unemployed father gets a job working for Will's father, and she responds not with gratitude but with anger that Will has tried to improve her life by making her family less dependent on her income. This anger, she begins to realize, makes her more sympathetic to what Will feels like when everything is being done for him. Lou's relationship with her boyfriend becomes increasingly strained, partly because her thoughts are ever more focused on Will, but also because she finds that her boyfriend, obsessed about his fitness regime, has no notion of how simply to be with her – which makes her reflect ruefully on whether she's been any more successful at learning genuinely to be with Will. When her boyfriend and Will finally meet, she's furious with her boyfriend as he's only able to relate to Will in a way that gives advice on body-strengthening; he is unable to see the person beyond the physical paralysis. The irony is that she hasn't been any different for most of her time in the job. Will, who likes to call her Clark, starts to question her about her reluctance to make more of her abilities – 'Your life's even duller than mine,' he says – which leads her to divulge a sexual assault that took place in her late adolescence that cursed her with such a catastrophic loss of confidence that she became in some ways as paralysed as her patient.

When Will gets a visit from a lawyer, a little detective work leads Lou to discover that Will is putting his affairs in order because he's planning to travel to Switzerland to be assisted to die. Lou realizes that she's a tool: her employment is the result of a bargain between Will and his mother. Will promised to delay his suicide by six months and his mother hired someone to cheer him up, hoping he'd change his mind. As Lou and Will become more fond of one another, Lou dreams up and executes the perfect plan. She takes Will on a once-in-a-lifetime exotic beachside holiday, hoping to deepen their relationship, inspire him with the beauty of living, and put out of his head all morbid thoughts of the Swiss clinic. On their last night, planning to spend the dark hours with him and express their budding love, Lou stands on the brink of triumph, but Will shatters her exaltation – he still intends to travel to Switzerland shortly after their return from their island paradise. Despite her utter dismay, Will insists. He is defined by his chair. She can see past it; he can't – or won't. This is his explanation:

> 'You never saw me before this thing. I loved my life, Clark. Really loved it. I loved my job, my travels, the things I was. I loved being a physical person. I liked riding my motorbike, hurling myself off buildings. I liked crushing people in business deals. I liked having sex. Lots of sex. I led a big life . . .

'It's not a matter of not giving you a chance. I've watched you these six months becoming a whole different person, someone who is only just beginning to see her possibilities. You have no idea how happy that has made me . . . I don't want you to be tied to me, to my hospital appointments, to the restrictions of my life . . .

'I don't want to look at you every day, to see you naked . . . and not be able to do what I want to do to you right now . . . I can't be the kind of man who just . . . accepts . . .

'I need it to end here. No more chair. No more pneumonia. No more burning limbs. No more pain and tiredness and waking up every morning already wishing it was over. When we get back, I am still going to go to Switzerland. And if you do love me, Clark, as you say you do, the thing that would make me happier than anything is if you would come with me.' (pp. 426–7)

Lou is shattered, and spends the journey home thinking, 'Why is this not enough for you? Why am I not enough for you?' She longs to have more time, and is dismayed that he didn't confide in her earlier. Her anger and hurt get the better of her and she refuses to see him in his last days, until a phone call from Will's mother in Switzerland begging her to come persuades her; and that trip to the Swiss bedside creates a poignant frame for the story. The novel began with a prologue in which Will and his then-girlfriend Alicia, deep under the duvet, doubtless exhausted from the best sex the world has ever known, oversleep. Realizing he is late, Will dresses rapidly before rushing out into the street – to come face to face with the reckless motorbike that all but kills him. The novel ends in a very different bedroom, with Will and a different girlfriend, one who has learnt that she can't give him what he most wants, but is nonetheless beside him to the last, as he faces a death of his own choosing.

The title *Me Before You* suggests a story about how people change from the person they were before they met each other; to some extent it is about how Will finds himself incapable of showing the selflessness towards Lou that she shows towards him. But the real story is how Lou comes clumsily and painfully to discover what it really means to stand before Will. It means realizing that you can't fix someone else's life; you won't necessarily succeed in cheering other people up by being a performing clown or party organizer; and a true relationship can't be based on one person's plenty and another person's lack. Will and Lou only find a relationship when they realize that they're both paralysed, and Lou only gives Will what he really needs when she sits beside his bed in Switzerland and stops trying to be the angel whose magic wand turns all to gold. Will's real problem isn't his quadriplegia; it's his fantasy of an eternal youth of perpetual energy, sensation and consumption, a fantasy he's obdurately determined to hold on to, even though Lou is clearly offering him something immeasurably more mature, sustainable and relational.

I want now to set this story of Lou Clark and Will Traynor alongside the account of Bryan Stevenson and Walter McMillian, in the context of what it means to be with a neighbour.

The biggest contrast between the two stories is that Bryan chooses to work on behalf of Walter. Walter makes the original contact, but by the time he does so Bryan has already been working for two years as a lawyer determined to get justice and release for prisoners on death row who have no reason to be there. Bryan has oriented his life in the direction of meeting someone like Walter. By contrast, Louisa Clark has, at the outset, no desire whatsoever to meet, let alone care for, Will Traynor. The class issues are reversed – in Bryan's case, while from a humble background he is a Harvard Law School graduate coming on to the territory of struggling folk in southern Alabama; in Lou's case, she is an underachieving, ambitionless young working-class woman coming on to the territory of a family that until two years before had exuded effortless perfection, whose affluence reduces her to feeling like an awkward intruder. The difference here is that Lou's neighbourliness is literal – she simply has no choice but to find a way to connect with Will, surly, miserable and rude as he is. Walter, by contrast, is Bryan's neighbour of choice, which is a different thing.

But there's a fascinating similarity. Earlier I suggested that what makes the word 'neighbour' so terrifying is that it seems to open the door to impossible demand. What seems special about Bryan, besides his evident legal genius and relentless appetite for work, is that he apparently can live with what to most of us would be an indescribable level of demand. He details the countless people on death row, the limitless flaws and shameful faults in the American legal system, the endless line of wrongful convictions and stitched-up sentences. He relates the times he's been overcome by tears as the horror of execution or the fury of corruption sinks in. But he never seems to stop. What seems so different about Lou is that she's the girl next door – living in the shadow of a more talented sister, struggling to sustain her impoverished family, quite content with her colourless boyfriend, with no desire to leave town or go to college or see the world. But by the end of the story she's even more overwhelmed by one neighbour than Bryan is by scores. Leaving the romantic dimension to one side, the lesson seems to be that if you're fully committed to be with even one person, in all their struggle and complexity, that commitment will overwhelm you quite as much as a commitment to be with everybody. It only takes one neighbour, and attention to their true need, to search the deepest recesses of your soul.

And another apparent difference leads to a second stirring similarity. Bryan is highly qualified: he's got family experience of violent death, since his grandfather was murdered during a bungled burglary; he's been to college and is a trained lawyer; and he's done serious time with the Southern Center for Human Rights, based in Atlanta, Georgia, before setting up his own non-profit organization in Montgomery, Alabama. He becomes a professor at New York University. Lou is not remotely qualified. Our first meeting with her details what she does know – and it starts with the number of steps from the bus stop to home. Her ambition is fulfilled in working at the local café. When she works for the Traynors, it's clear that the physiotherapist does the heavy lifting, in every sense: she's just there to check that Will doesn't find a way to slit his wrists. When Lou does try to do something for Will, like take him to the races, it's generally a humiliating failure.

It seems that Bryan and Lou are opposites. But they both make the same discovery. When Lou shares her point of real pain with Will, a genuine mutuality begins to arise, where both begin to see how trapped they each are, and how the other one is offering a key that could perhaps give them release. Likewise, what Bryan discovers is that the real joys of his job lie in the kind of fellowship and reciprocity he establishes with Walter and the camaraderie he shares with Walter's wider family. And by the end of his memoir, the lessons he has learnt are not about his triumphs and victories but about his own brokenness and the fact that there's something deeper than justice, and that's mercy – because after all the anger and hurt and discrimination and cruelty and humiliation, you have to find a way to go on living, and ultimately that means showing mercy to those who scarcely for one moment deserve it. Just as Lou discovers that being a true neighbour to even one person opens a vast canyon of impossible demand, such that her neighbourliness and that of Bryan Stevenson are of the same quality despite their many circumstantial differences, so all four of the people in question – Walter, Bryan, Lou and Will – find respectively that their common humanity as neighbours lies in their brokenness.

The word 'neighbour' is a rather antiquated term except in one context: seeking to live the parable of the Good Samaritan. Elsewhere I have suggested that the best exegesis of the parable is to understand that the Samaritan is Jesus. And this provides the key that releases the identity and potential of the neighbour. If we see ourselves as the neighbour, the world looks the same as it does to the optician of Lampedusa: an ocean of impossible demand. But if we see the neighbour as Jesus, our perspective is transformed and the neighbour becomes the one who is coming to give us gifts, wisdom, insight, blessing – in short, coming to save us. It is Jesus, rather than we, who regards the whole earth as a neighbour and doesn't turn away from us in the anger and hurt and discrimination and cruelty and humiliation we inflict or receive; who is our advocate when we walk through the valley of the shadow of death, whether by our own or another's folly; and who waits by the bedside of our wrong choices and in the confusion of our clumsy forms of love.

Jojo Moyes's novel *Me Before You* might just as well be a theological story in which Will discovers that Jesus is not the neighbour who fixes his problems or cheers him up but who abides with him in his heart of darkness and shapes his whole life so as never to let him go. And Bryan Stevenson's memoir *Just Mercy* might equally be a theological account of how we have a high priest who not only meets us in our brokenness but is able to speak with us about sports, TV, popular culture, or anything else we want to discuss, and who weeps when we face punishment and knows sorrows just like our own. We do have an advocate with the Father who is our neighbour in heaven and whose Spirit infuses each one of our neighbours on earth.

Towards the end of *Just Mercy*, Bryan Stevenson recalls how on the steps of a courthouse he met an older black lady wearing a 'church meeting hat'. She said, 'My 16-year-old grandson was murdered 15 years ago, and I loved that boy more than life itself.' Some boys were found guilty for killing her grandson. She thought that their conviction would make her feel better but actually it made her feel worse. A woman came over as the trial concluded and encouraged her to lean on her shoulder. The woman asked if the boys convicted were hers, and the older lady said no, the boy they killed was hers. Then she said:

> 'I think she sat with me for almost two hours. For well over an hour, we didn't neither of us say a word. It felt good to finally have someone to lean on at that trial, and I've never forgotten that woman . . . About a year later I started coming down here. I don't really know why. I guess I felt like maybe I could be someone, that somebody hurting could lean on . . .

> 'When I first came, I'd look for people who had lost someone to murder or some violent crime. Then it got to the point where some of the ones grieving the most were the ones whose children or parents were on trial, so I just started letting anyone lean on me who needed it. All these young children being sent to prison forever, all this grief and violence. Those judges throwing people away like they're not even human, people shooting each other, hurting each other like they don't care. I don't know, it's a lot of pain. I decided that I was supposed to be here to catch some of the stones people cast at each other.'

Then she said to Bryan, 'I heard you in that courtroom today. I've even seen you here a couple of times before. I know you're a stonecatcher, too' (pp. 307–9).

That's what neighbours do. Catch stones – and sit for two hours as a shoulder to lean on. The first, catching stones, is what Jesus did on the cross. The second, coming to us and offering us a shoulder to lean on, is what he does for ever. Bryan is a stonecatcher; Lou is a shoulder. Together they demonstrate what it means to be with the neighbour.

Notes

1 Emma Jane Kirby, *The Optician of Lampedusa* (London: Penguin, 2016), pp. 27–8.
2 Bryan Stevenson, *Just Mercy: A Story of Justice and Redemption* (New York: Random House, 2014). Paginations in text.
3 Jojo Moyes, *Me Before You* (London: Penguin, 2012, also a 2016 film). Paginations in text.

Epilogue: My neighbour in Trafalgar Square

Richard Carter

When I first came to live in Trafalgar Square I thought I would never be able to sleep. This city never stops. I come home at night, stepping respectfully and guiltily over the night's occupant of our doorstep. By 2 a.m. most of the revellers and club-goers have made their noisy way past, and the buskers have called it a day, but now the drunken arguments and swearing outside my window have begun. Though I have pulled the curtains and turned off the lights, my bedroom is bright with streetlights and the flashing revolving lights of street cleaning trucks with their spinning brushes and reversing bleeps, and the noise of refuse trucks emptying bottle banks with the roar of smashing glass. Across my ceiling flashing blue is the incessant wailing of police, fire and ambulance sirens – and by the time all this has finished the sun is rising. At first I tried to block out the city. How could I find my sanctuary, my place of holiness, in the midst of all of this? Of course, I had not realized that this city was my sanctuary and those walking past would become my neighbours.

I always remember the words I heard from Rowan Williams that he preached at the 2008 Lambeth Conference as bishops from the Anglican Communion gathered from around the world, each bringing their own painful struggles, prejudices and divisions. Here in the centre of London these words have never left me:

> Each person is diminished by the pain of another person and enriched by the holiness of another and if we say that we no longer can hear the pain of another, we can no longer feel empathy with a homeless man in London, an asylum seeker seeking a safe home, a mother and her family threatened by global warming, a political prisoner beaten with sticks because he has voted for the opposition, or a sinner who has lost the way: if our church is not living this connectedness with humanity then God forgive us and help us for we have lost Christ the Word who became flesh and lived among us . . . This is unity, this is our calling – to let the Son of God be revealed in us, to be a sign of a unity that brings alive that deep connectedness in the human world.

Who is my neighbour? Let me reflect on a few encounters during a week in Trafalgar Square.

Monday

> A man was going down from Jerusalem to Jericho and fell into the hands of robbers, who stripped him, beat him, and went away leaving him half dead. (Luke 10.30)

It had begun with her falling in love against the advice of her parents. This act of disobedience, she believed, had had catastrophic consequences, so that now as she looked back it appeared to be the cause of years of suffering. I do not want to describe what she told me in detail lest I give the evil more substance and permanence before we, as it were, walk by on the other side of the road. Suffice it to say, it included unimaginable violence against her and her children carried out by her partner – torture, beatings, humiliation, slicing with blades, rape – and then, when she escaped, destitution, loneliness, guilt and then further entrapment through trafficking by another man unbelievably even worse than the first, as though passed on from one evil to another. And the fear within her that because of her that same suffering she has known will be visited upon the next generation. The person beaten and left for dead on the road to Jericho is not a thing of the past. Sometimes it would even appear better to be dead. 'It is my destiny to suffer,' she said. 'No, no,' I tried to convince her, 'it is not,' and then summoning up the only words that would come into my head: 'God loves you.' I meant it, meant it with all my heart. After her story I longed to believe it. 'God loves you.' But now her pain had become a scream, ripped from her guts – a guttural primordial cry of anguish. I have heard that cry before and there is no mistaking it, for it comes from the horror of having seen evil face to face. 'Is this God's love? Is this what you call God's love? How can you say God loves me? Is this life of mine – is this God's love? Is this God's love?'

God's love powerless, immobile, found wanting. God's love nailed to a cross.

I am defenceless, silenced by her cry. After those words there can be no pretending. All I know is that somehow God's love is this woman's courage; her love, her scream, her longing for resurrection, Christ's cry that it is finished – no more suffering, no more humiliation or pain. 'God loves you.' I knew it to be true. Naked truth, without explanation. The only thing worth believing in. And I knew as I have often known in my life that this woman is both the one who was beaten and left for dead on the road to Jericho and also the Good Samaritan. Because the one thing that is most astonishing in this parable is that the Good Samaritan is the very last person you expect to be the Good Samaritan. There, in Jesus' day, even putting those words together – 'good' and 'Samaritan' – would have appeared an impossibility, and yet they were a truth. We part but her memory does not depart. It haunts me, pursues me and cries: 'How can you say God loves me?'

Tuesday

Now by chance a priest was going down that road; and when he saw him, he passed by on the other side.
(Luke 10.31)

Sometimes the need just seems too great. We don't pass by because we don't care. We pass by because we do care but don't know what to do. And if we were to get involved, what then? There is no easy solution or answer. Better not to get involved at all than simply to open up this ocean of need. Won't it be like opening a wound? I've tried before – I really have. I've helped others, and not walked by, but I can't do it every night. No bed for the night that I can instantly summon up and pay the bill. There is no visa, no right to remain, no job waiting for you to begin, no housing, no hostel in Westminster willing to take you this late at night. And if I were to stop I know I would discover a life

I cannot solve, a need I cannot provide for, or a suffering I cannot face at this time of night. And so with utmost respect I step over this man on my doorstep, trying to get my keys in the lock of my front door without disturbing him, and to lift my bicycle over his curled-up body in the thin sleeping bag. He stirs and lifts his head, looking up at me. 'Sorry to disturb you,' I say respectfully as I stagger through the door into the light, warmth and safety of the house. If I were to let him in, what then? I think it would not end there. There would be another person on my doorstep tomorrow. The whole house would become quickly filled with unanswerable need. How would I ever do my job?

We often fear those we do not know. The Jews would have feared the Gentiles. The Gentiles would have feared the Jews. Yet in our parable fear becomes the opportunity for mercy. The Spirit of God is the Spirit of mercy. The parable of the Good Samaritan is a parable about mercy. But mercy is costly. It can't be embarked upon lightly.

Around Trafalgar Square there are many lives you long to save. The busker who looks a bit like Ralph McTell is singing outside my window about 'the old man'. I've seen him many times, and the old girl with carrier bags. In fact I've just stepped over one of them on my doorstep. In the morning another homeless man walks past me as I go over to open up the church. His hood is up, his coat stiff with the grime of living on the streets, a black noble face. No carrier bags – he pulls a heavy suitcase, the wheels buckled and useless, so the metal edges of the suitcase are noisily dragging along the pavement. I think that all he has is here. It's like a huge dragged burden – a weight to pull with no future.

The suitcase is not a sign of possession but the label of dispossession. And I bleed inwardly for him, wounded by the sound of those scraping, broken wheels. I imagine for a moment the journey that has brought him here. The hope contained in a packed suitcase and now the humiliation – this arrival in our nation, inflicted upon him like a ball and chain. This Kafkaesque labyrinth of unwelcome. The road that doesn't lead to Jericho but to the side of the road. And I long for his freedom and mine. For we both have baggage we drag, and long for release. 'Good morning,' I say. But he doesn't reply.

Straight after prayer a woman is waiting in the church. 'Can I have a word?' she asks. She moves in like an iceberg – only a little bit of the need is visible but the unseen is ready to sink you. Yes, you can have a word, I think, but I haven't got space to carry it. I can't save you or heal the wound in your eyes. Yes, I want to help, but the need is too big. I want to pacify my guilt at arm's distance. To leave the black bin liner of old clothes at the refuge but then go home.

This morning there is a meeting. I am in a crowded room full of priests, but the person I am talking to is not really listening to me. It's as if there are cataracts in his eyes. I am speaking to him about refugees. He is looking at me blankly – or is it past me to the next conversation? He moves on, smiling benevolently in the way priests do when they want to get away. How often have I used that same smile?

Each Tuesday I meet a group of homeless people, or at least people who have known homelessness, at The Connection at St Martin's for what we call 'Spiritual Space'. The Connection is both a day centre and an emergency night shelter for homeless and vulnerably housed people. It aims to support people out of homelessness. It is used by about 4,000 people a year. 'Why do you call us homeless people?' I remember Lesley asking in one of my first groups when we began Spiritual Space about seven years ago. 'I mean, I don't call you in-house people. We are all just people.' The day I began the group, it felt like me against them. They asked me every question Christianity struggles with. Why doesn't God answer my prayers? Why is God punishing me? Why do priests abuse children? Why are Christians hypocrites? Why doesn't the Church do more to help? Will I go to hell for the things I've done wrong? Why doesn't God do something to change the evils of our world? After an hour and a half I staggered out of Spiritual Space. I knew that things would have to change. I could not provide the answers, but we could share the questions and create space for listening and, I believe, for God: God in one another.

One Tuesday at Spiritual Space we were talking about the Spirit of God. Had we ever in our lives had an experience of that Holy Spirit? One member of the group told us that although he was homeless he had always kept in his bag a pair of roller blades. 'The wheels are no good now,' he said, 'but I still keep them. One day I will get them mended, because when I put them on I feel like a bird and I am free.' Stuart said, 'You don't want to hear about my life – everything is f***** up. I've never experienced God's Spirit, only evil spirits.' Then the woman next to him said, 'I experienced God's Spirit when I gave birth to my daughter and held her in my hands. I just couldn't believe it.' This seemed to awaken Stuart's own experience because suddenly he started to talk, to explain about his girlfriend and how she had got pregnant and how the baby was premature; how he had been the only one there and it was too late to get her to hospital and he'd had to help her – help the baby out with his own hands, with the umbilical cord and all, holding the baby in his hands. He said that his baby daughter was a fighter; she was so beautiful. After the group Stuart came to me and told me how he'd done so many things wrong and he felt that he should be punished, but this daughter was the most precious thing in his whole life. It was a confession pouring out of him and he asked what his punishment would be. I said to him the thought that came from within me: 'Your penance is to love your daughter.' A week later he returned to see me. 'Loving my daughter is not a punishment,' he told me. 'I thought that penance was meant to be a punishment . . . I don't want mercy, I want punishment.'

For what? So he could continue beating up himself and everyone else? So he could continue being the victim, who'd messed up his life and got things wrong? That was going to do a lot of good. Perhaps the courage is in accepting you can be forgiven and all that entails. Real courage is in the transformation of your life by God's love. I can't do that. I've gone too far wrong. Three times Peter betrayed him. Three times Jesus asks Peter, who had deserted him, 'Do you love me?' Three times he tells him: 'Then feed my sheep.'

Your penance is to love. Your penance is mercy. The mercy of God. We might be the man injured on the road. We might be the thief who injures. We might be those who walk past on the other side. We might be all of these. But the journey is to become the Good Samaritan – to recognize how to love our neighbour and in so doing to love ourselves.

Who is teaching whom?

Wednesday

So likewise a Levite, when he came to the place and saw him, passed by on the other side.   (Luke 10.32)

On Wednesday I visited the prison. I went by tube, walked down Henchman Street, to what is known as the Scrubs – Wormwood Scrubs: like a name from gothic horror. The high walls, barbed wire, the huge dark Victorian brick buildings with their long lime-green painted corridors. Outside the first wing I could hear shouts coming from the windows. 'That's where the new arrivals are put,' the chaplain told me. 'A lot of them are scared when they first arrive.' I imagined how scared I would be. The enclosure below the wing was full of litter dropped from the windows. Recently there had been a lockdown and they had been kept in their cells for 23 hours a day. We often define people by their crimes. 'Oh, he's a category B prisoner,' or 'He's in for violent assault' – or theft or drugs or whatever. Actually, when you meet people doing time inside prison the first thing that strikes you is that they are not categories at all. They are, as Lesley said, 'all just people', many of them very young people. 'I've been in five different prisons,' said one young man who looked barely older than 25. 'This is the last time, though. I'm going to go straight.' I hoped so. I really did. I felt a longing for these young guys to be free – free not only of this prison, with people caged like battery hens, but free of those cycles of crime that lead to over 70 per cent reoffending and being put back in prison.

I wonder how I would manage in one of those cells. Two bunk beds, a toilet, hardly room to turn round. Things have hardly changed since *Papillon*. If I didn't have problems before I went into a cell like that, I certainly would by the time I came out. They do. I think of all the guilt and the shame and the longing and the anger and broken relationships that would fester in that confinement. I think of Christ wanting to gather his children under his wings – how much more his longing for all those at Wormwood Scrubs. In the kitchen I chat for a long time to an 'inmate'. 'I am a chef,' he said. 'I'm here for five years – the food's rubbish.' He shows me a plastic bag with some oats, a small carton of milk and a bread roll. 'That's my breakfast and lunch. I just want to do my time here. Keep my head down and get out. Pray for me, Father.' Strange how present God feels. So many people longing for another chance at life. I think of the Levite walking by on the other side of the road.

Thursday

But a Samaritan while travelling came near him . . .
(Luke 10.33)

I went to Honor Oak Crematorium to take the funeral of John Brian Murphy. Brian, as I called him, did not come to the services at St Martin's much, but most Sundays he came to the tea and coffee in the hall afterwards, where he sat on the same table with his group of friends: Jim, Patrick, Bush and John Davies. When I arrived at the crematorium there was no one there. And when the undertakers arrived with the coffin they asked if anyone else was coming. 'I hope so,' I said. I had never been to a funeral where no one came, and it seemed sad. But then an older gentleman arrived who said he was there for Brian's funeral. 'I'm the one John always called the Man with No Name,' he said, 'because at the café where we drank tea together the waitress would never say hello to me, so Brian started calling me the Man with No Name and it stuck.'

'I think we'd better begin,' said the undertaker.

'I think we'd better wait for John Davies,' I said. 'He must be coming; he made the arrangements.'

'Oh, you mean the one Brian always called Global Warming,' said the Man with No Name.

'Yes,' I said, recalling my weekly conversations on the portico with John about climate change. And sure enough, in the distance, making their way towards the crematorium, were two figures. 'That's Global Warming,' said the Man with No Name.

And the other one striding towards us with ski poles was Alastair Anson. I could have hugged him. Alastair, aged 87, ex-Royal Navy, former churchwarden, heart of gold; I was so pleased he had turned up.

'Oh yes, it's the Commander,' said the Man with no Name.

And so the four of us together remembered the life of John Brian Murphy. His childhood in Mossley Hill, Liverpool, his degree in history at Cambridge, his struggles with unemployment, depression and homelessness, his love for his partner Ellen who died in 1999 – his love of politics, his generosity and friendliness, and the way he was always ready to share a cup of tea. Suddenly the day seemed transformed – the sun came out and shone through the window on to the coffin, John spoke with warmth about his friend's generous spirit, Alastair read the lesson, I told Brian's story, and Elgar's 'Nimrod' played as the coffin disappeared. After the funeral I suggested we go for a cup of tea. Brian would like that. And so we went for a cuppa together in the local café, and spent an hour chatting about Brian and his life and kindness. I looked around the table at this unlikely group of Good Samaritans – the Man with No Name, Global Warming, the Commander, and of course John Brian Murphy, who felt so present. 'Actually,' they told me, 'we didn't call him Brian. We used to call him Strider, because he walked so fast.' Strider, who had gone on ahead of us from Jerusalem to Jericho. 'I'll pay for this,' said the Commander. 'That's what Strider would have done,' said the Man with No Name, 'picked up the bill. Though he never had any money for himself.'

Friday

And when he saw him, he was moved . . .

(Luke 10.33)

Friday is my day off, so I go to visit my mother. 'How is your mother?' people ask kindly. I never know what to say. I could say she has dementia. But that never seems adequate – as though I am confining her to a diagnostic category. As though the description diminishes her and all

that she was and is to those who love her. To say she has
dementia defines symptoms, or defines by defect, but it does
not define her personhood. 'How's your mother?' So I say
in reply, 'She has ups and downs – we love her a lot.' We do.
I can only speak of her by relationship. For several months
she has been very quiet when I go to visit; not saying more
than a couple of words, not responding to questions or
saying goodbye when I leave. This leaves me feeling empty
and bereft. Yet she is still so much my mother. My mother,
concentrated – all that she has ever been, distilled – her
frustration, her moments of despair, her flashes of anger,
her strength, her kindness, her poetry, her touches of spite,
her need for attention, and her deep love for people and for
me. On Friday we sit together quietly – and then, like an
awakening, she talks. She tells me it's not easy not being able
to move or do anything for herself. 'It's like being in exile.'

'I wonder how it could be made more bearable?' I ask her.

'I'd like to go shopping,' she says. 'And feed Charlie myself
[that's her dog]. And I'd like to write some letters to my
friends who I miss. I say my prayers, but with this pain I
sometimes find it hard to believe in God. Is that wrong?'
she asks.

'No, I don't think it is. I think it's very understandable. Even
Jesus found it hard to believe in God when he was in pain,'
I reply.

In the afternoon I take her to Kew Gardens and push her in
her wheelchair. The daffodils are coming out, and there are
carpets of blue violets. 'Is that a nest in the top of that tree?'

she asks. It is. The signs of new life are all around us. In the café she asks if she can have a cappuccino. 'Of course,' I say, delighted. 'It's really delicious,' she says.

Back home, I say prayers with her. It has been the most wonderful day. When my brother gets home from work, he phones to tell me that Mum's written three letters from her chair. 'You can't read what she's written,' he says. 'Her writing is too small and unsteady, but as she wrote them she talked about each one.'

'You must send them,' I said. 'The words don't matter. Her love is in the action.'

I am made so aware that God is not something formulaic or a theory. It is much more that we are the beloved of God. We cannot be defined by the categories we create – they seem almost like blasphemies against the life of God in us. A life that is so much more. We are not 'its', we are 'thous'. We are not objects, we are God's children – we have souls. Souls, whether living in this world or the next, whether prisoners or free, whether in sickness or in health. Think of all the times we treat others as if they are 'its' without souls, objects – the homeless, or the trafficked, or the abused, or criminals, or sex offenders, or victims, or the unemployed, or gypsies, or homosexuals, or Eastern Europeans, or schizophrenics, or those with dementia. And by treating others as 'its', we deny the means that God gave us all to seek salvation. The difference between an 'it' and a 'thou' is in the relationship. That is the source of our salvation. God's relationship with us. When we find our neighbour we find God. All of us are capable of creating 'its' – turning people into outsiders, even our own parents. Members of the European Union can become 'its'. Is not Europe also our neighbour? And what about those we call asylum seekers and migrants – that huge migration of those fleeing war or poverty and seeking a better life? Once human beings are positioned as outsiders, as nothing more than examples of a diagnostic category, or sickness, or problem, or fear, then their essential humanity, their personhood, is lost, and they become threats . . . they become Samaritans.

Yet is it not in these places of abandonment – on the cross, outside a city wall, on the road to Jericho, places that we too often inhabit – that we also can come face to face with the love of God? Is it not here that Christ calls us each by name, whether Lesley or Strider or Global Warming or the Commander or the Man with No Name or the chef in Wormwood Scrubs or my dear mother? Is it not here that we are given the opportunity to learn to love our neighbour as we love ourselves?

Saturday

He went to him and bandaged his wounds, having poured oil and wine on them. (Luke 10.34)

The Good Samaritan did not know that he was the Good Samaritan. Good Samaritans rarely do. He simply did it. He was just a Samaritan. If you had told him that people would be telling his story for the next 2,000 years he would have thought you were joking. Good Samaritans don't help the other because they want to become a parable. They do it because that's the only thing they can do. Often it goes unnoticed, or is just taken for granted. The simple act of goodness that can change water into wine and the guests don't even know where the wine has come from. But sometimes things happen. Things that are so big they make others think and take account. Saturday is a day for big events in Trafalgar Square – protests, celebrations, national days, Pride, demonstrations. 'Hello, London!' Each Saturday I hear a different person on a microphone announce the words as if they are the first. But there are public events you never forget. At a vigil in Trafalgar Square for Jo Cox, a young mother, a compassionate and by all accounts inspirational politician, brutally murdered in the deluded name of patriotism, the words of this poem by Dorothy Oger were read:

For love
I shall stand for love,
Even with a broken soul,
Even with a heavy heart.

I shall stand for love,
For the world is wounded.
Not just my little piece of land,
Where I am mostly safe,
Where I am mostly well,
But our world, everywhere
Every day.

I shall stand for love,
Because we need more light,
Not more deaths,
Not more power,
Not more bombs.

I shall stand for love,
So that our children are safe
So that our friends are sheltered
So that our borders are open.

I shall stand for love,
Even with a broken soul,
Even with a heavy heart.
(Dorothy Oger, Brussels, 23 March 2016)

There was a crowd of thousands, and as we heard the words of this poem there was total silence. 'I shall stand for love.' I scribbled the words down on my hand. I knew they were important, worth writing down; more than that, as the life of Jo Cox testified, worth giving one's life for. I shall stand for love.

I was particularly struck by the second line. 'I shall stand for love, even with a broken soul, even with a heavy heart.' We often, of course, think of love as the end of the film – the unity that you romantically reach as the music swells. But the truth is that it's often when our souls are broken open and our hearts are heavy that we have to work out and make the choice – where do we stand and what are we prepared to stand for? Like now – standing for love now even with a broken soul and a heavy heart. It is actually at this very point that the Christian faith in fact makes most sense. Is it not Christ who remains the constant? Like an anchor deeper than the sea? Like the rock on which to build the Church? 'I shall stand for love.'

After the result of the European referendum, our vicar Sam wrote to the staff and congregation of St Martin's – a gathered community here in the centre of London from so many parts of the world, with many from Europe, all such integral parts of this place. At the end of that letter he said:

> We believe it's possible to build together a community of humility, generosity, gratitude, grace, truth and compassion – for which the only word we know is church. We're called to be a living example of what the reconciling, liberating and transforming love of God can do. It may be that a witness like ours can begin to heal our country and inspire it to take a different, more inclusive and more hopeful direction. But if it does not, we are going to do it anyway.

The Good Samaritan stood for love. But probably at the time he wouldn't have thought about standing for anything. It was just there inside him, an instinct. When we meet the reality, we don't ask ourselves, 'Shall I help a Jew or shall I help a Gentile?' We think, 'Quick! This person needs help. Am I going to let him die or am I going to do something?'

Love for neighbour is not a moral commandment to which we adhere in order to gain virtue or holiness. Love takes our neighbour as our other self (for this neighbour could so easily have been us), and is present to him or her without judgement, and with discretion, humility and reverence. Our lives are with our neighbours, whoever they may be. In discovering our neighbour we discover God. And when we become by God's gift a means of connecting another with God, we have become the gospel.

I remember when we held prayers for a same-sex partnership at St Martin's, there in the congregation was Gloria. Gloria, who had always, at every opportunity, voiced her opposition to homosexuality. 'I didn't expect to see you, Gloria. I'm so pleased you've come,' I said. 'What do you mean?' said Gloria. 'It's for Adam and Tony. I love Tony and Adam. I wouldn't miss being here for anything.' I shall stand for love.

Sunday

'Take care of him; and when I come back, I will repay you whatever more you spend.'   (Luke 10.35)

He wears a black woollen cap pulled down over his hair. I once saw him take it off and glimpsed the plaits beneath; but perhaps he feels his hair is too matted or knotted by the rain. He doesn't speak much. It is his actions that speak. And slowly, over the weeks, he has lifted up his eyes, and his face has lit up into a smile and his kindness has filled the place. He came as a guest to our International Group – a place where we offer hospitality to those without recourse to public funds and end up discovering the hospitality they offer to us, so that we are no longer sure who is the guest and who is the host. It began with the washing up – simply, quietly taking control of dirty dishes, washing and rinsing at speed, laughing when I tried to help. The sink becoming the place of hospitality and meeting – washing away the mess and grease, plunging into clean water. Then he began on the pots, the serving trays, the surfaces, the serving counters – cleaning so everything gleamed, clearing away, putting back – his smile and laugh radiating outwards. He galvanized us.

Sunday after Sunday, the quietest became the one we all depended on most, the one whose presence inspired us all. As we carry huge bags of rice back from Chinatown, he hurries on ahead of me with his two bags, and before I am halfway back he has returned empty-handed to help me carry mine. Walking 74 miles to Canterbury on our annual pilgrimage, when we, the slowest group of pilgrims, have staggered into the church halls in the evenings, he has reached there three hours before, sorted our luggage, and found our sleeping bags and a place to sleep. Nothing servile – but brave, self-sufficient, strong. This man has crossed Africa, spent time working to raise money for his passage in Libya, crossed the Mediterranean in a boat that almost sank, crossed Europe, spent months in the Calais Jungle, getting to the UK God knows how. He has a kindness and an awareness of the needs of others that staggers. And yet he is so self-contained, demanding nothing – just this instinctive giving of self. He is 'fit': fit of mind, fit of body, fit of attitude; he fits the group. Without complaint, without request, without moan, without profit, without motive: he generously gives and we are made richer by his presence. He is the beloved disciple.

A tourist once entered our church and asked me loudly: 'Who are all these mummies in your church?' I didn't know what he meant at first. Then he pointed to all the hooded or blanketed sleeping people who sit in the box pews around the edges of our church. 'This lot – these mummies.'

I was outraged. 'These people are my community,' I wanted to say. Their snoring is part of our prayers. Every morning when we open up, there they are waiting to come into the church, and I never cease to be amazed at their graciousness and good spirits after a night on the streets, offering to help push the heavy metal gates open. During the renewal and renovation of the church, one of them said to me: 'I hope this is not going to be like a pub make-over. I mean, this is our church. We spend more time in it than you do.' They do. They are a constant reminder that this is why we are here. That the church is not just some club for its private members, or even worse a tourist shrine – it is the home of all. These people are the church, just as we are. A church grounded in the reality of people's lives. They make us remember the vision of Dick Sheppard all those years ago – the priest who was the Good Samaritan, and at times of depression and despair in his own life, the one who needed a Samaritan too. Returning from the trauma of the trenches, he described his vision, a vision that has animated this place and by God's grace will go on animating it in its service for decades, or even please God centuries, to come.

This is what he said:

I stood on the West steps and saw what this church would be to the life of the people. They passed me, into its warm inside, hundreds and hundreds of all sorts of people, going up to the temple of their Lord, with all their difficulties, trials and sorrows. I saw it full of people, dropping in at all hours of the day and night. It was never dark, it was lighted all night and all day, and often and often tired bits of humanity swept in. And I said to them as they passed: 'Where are you going?' And they said only one thing, 'This is our home. This is where we are going to learn of the love of Jesus

Christ. This is the altar of our Lord where all our peace lies. This is St Martin's.' It was all reverent and full of love and they never pushed me behind a pillar because I was poor. And day by day they told me the dear Lord's Supper was there on his altar waiting to be given. They spoke to me two words only, one was the word 'home' and the other was 'love'.

Is this realizable or is it just sentimental? What I wanted to do was shout at that tourist. I wanted to tell him the names of those around the edges and their gifts and their qualities and to suggest that many of them were closer to God than he was. The only reply that came into my head was, 'They are our neighbours.'

But could I claim this? Were they our neighbours? How many of us in the worshipping congregation knew their names? We were the church of the homeless and yet many of the homeless we knew very little about. And perhaps like many churches we often did not do anything because we were not quite sure what to do. We thought, like people often think, that we ought to do something for them yet we might not be able to solve their problems, so we did nothing. Many of those sleeping in our pews were those with no recourse to public funds and it would be true that if we tried to help them there would be no easy solutions to their difficulties. But was that an excuse to ignore their existence? Does the fact that someone has difficulties and we can't solve them prevent us from making relationships? I asked for volunteers among the congregation to discover whether anyone was willing to help provide hospitality for these people with no recourse to public funds. Forty people responded and in 2013 we founded the International Group, providing welcome for refugees and migrants who are facing destitution. It would not be an exaggeration to say that through this ministry we have discovered our neighbour, and our neighbour is no longer a person simply on the edge, but us, as we eat together, share together and offer one another the gifts of our hospitality. Who is the guest and who is the host? It is now difficult to tell.

We come from over 35 different countries. We speak many languages. We have experienced many different cultures. We come from different faiths, and also faithlessness. We each come with our own wounds, carrying the scars of our lives in our bodies and scorched in our memories. We carry our own hopes, our own achievements and insurmountable needs. We are different colours, ages, sexes, genders, sexualities. We don't know all the answers. We know our failings. Some of us have money to generously share, some of us don't, but all of us have something to give. The greatest poverty is to believe that you cannot help another, and it is a real truth that it is those who believe they have least who in fact often seem to have the grace to give the most. We all have the opportunity to be the Good Samaritan. That's the story. We come from many different places to this place where our journeys meet. Who are we? The truth is that we are all the body of Christ.

For Easter this year I wanted to make a Passion Play in which the gospel would come alive. Each week we gather in this church – those at the centre and those on the wings. But for this play it is those on the edges Christ calls to be his disciples. There is Mugisha, who sits at the back, who cared for an old man in his home for 15 years through his dementia, and when the man died his relatives, who had seldom visited, asked Mugisha to leave the house and so he became homeless. There is big Len, who sleeps in the streets at night, but is writing a book in the public library by day and is one of the wisest people I know. There is Edward, who is an actor and has written his own musical, but in just a few months seems to have aged 20 years on the streets, so that his face is now weary and his joints rusted by the cold, and each day his walking becomes more difficult. There is Anom, with his loving heart, disowned by his mother because he is gay, who has travelled from Indonesia, to the USA, to London, in search of himself, and has found himself and John and the God of love and all of us. If only his mother could recognize his grace and goodness rather than walking by on the other side in the name of her false god of shame, reputation and what the neighbours think. How proud she should be of his humanity. She is missing a gift of God. There is Edwin, the reflective chess champion – searching for the meaning of life. And there is, of course, the one with the black woollen hat pulled down. And there is Sam, who plays Jesus; he comes from Afghanistan and at this church has discovered the love of God. 'I don't want a God who creates half people. I want a God who creates us whole and wants everyone to be equal,' he told me when he first came to St Martin's. It's not been easy for him in the UK: arriving as a minor, learning a new culture on his own, beaten so badly in an unprovoked attack that he was almost blinded in one eye, learning how to love in a culture that seems at times impossibly confusing – free and yet controlled, compassionate yet hypocritical. The journey to the UK was a tough one. Perhaps the journey here in the UK is even tougher.

Christ's Passion has not ended. Our Jesus is not whipped but waterboarded. He is mocked by his captors, who strip him and dress him in an orange boiler suit and take selfies of his humiliation. Our Pilate asks with a New York accent, 'What is Truth?' The young innocent Jesus screams from the cross, 'My God, my God, why have you forsaken me?' Or is it, 'How can you say that God loves me?' The news, as it always is, has been horrifying. A young Kurdish Iranian asylum seeker is kicked unconscious by a mob in Croydon. Amo Singh, a shop keeper, is brutally assaulted and left for dead outside his shop in Stroud – after trying to prevent a gang attack against a Polish boy. And on a scale too terrifying to even grasp, horrifying images of the Syrian town of Khan Sheikhoun, with vivid news footage of dozens of people, many of them children, writhing, choking, foaming at the mouth, and dead, after breathing in poison after warplanes dropped bombs in the early morning hours. Meanwhile the UK paves the way for new trade deals with Saudi Arabia, whose war against Yemen has already claimed more than 10,000 civilian lives, resourced by a lucrative £3 billion arms deal with Britain. It is as though we, like the crowds in Jerusalem, have lost our moral compass.

It's Sunday but Good Friday continues – the innocent are still being put to death in our world. Yet is it not on this Golgotha that the gospel becomes something that is not an appendage to life but where our lives themselves are at stake? 'Father, forgive them, they do not know what they are doing.' Is it not here that the resurrection gift of peace becomes all that we long for? Melissa Cochran, interviewed about the death of her husband Kurt in the terrorist attack on Westminster Bridge, spoke about bearing no ill will towards his killer: 'All I know is that he did not have the beautiful heart my husband had and I am sorry for him.' There she sits with tears falling, renouncing the hatred that would prevent healing.

Our homeless disciples in our Passion Play come towards the crucified Christ in bewilderment, their arms reaching out towards his body. Then the one who has a black woollen hat pulled down over his head, this man who doesn't say much but speaks through his actions, takes Jesus down from the cross, cradles him in his arms so gently, places his body on the stone altar of our church with such compassion and respect. Has he done this before? Has he carried Christ? Yes, every week; we have seen him. Perhaps he learnt to carry Christ through the struggle and the pain. This is the beloved disciple who leaned in at Christ's side and upon whom God leans. Who is my neighbour? Is not this the one? The excluded one who has become our witness. And cannot we become this witness too? We who fear our own unworthiness. Cannot each one of us who comes to the altar find that the place of death can be transformed into the place of resurrection and love? 'The body of our Lord Jesus Christ which was broken for you preserve your body and soul into everlasting life.' Each and every broken one of us, Christ's body.

'Which of these three, do you think, was a neighbour to the man who fell into the hands of robbers?' He said, 'The one who showed him mercy.' Jesus said to him, 'Go and do likewise.' (Luke 10.36)

Printed and bound by CPI Group (UK) Ltd, Croydon, CR0 4YY

25/03/2025

14647344-0005